VICTORIAN PRESTON
AND THE
WHITTINGHAM
HOSPITAL RAILWAY

A Social History

Coronation Pacific No. 46234 *Duchess of Abercorn* and sister engine No. 46235 *City of Birmingham* make a fine sight at Preston station *c*. 1961. (Tony Gillett)

In commemoration of Preston Guild 2012 and the wonderful age of steam.

On 6 May 1961, Brittannia Pacific No. 70014 *Iron Duke* (already relegated from passenger duties) is seen with an up fully fitted freight passing Maudland Sidings, north of Preston station. (Tony Gillett)

VICTORIAN PRESTON

AND THE

WHITTINGHAM
HOSPITAL RAILWAY

David John Hindle MA

AMBERLEY

First published 2012

Amberley Publishing
The Hill, Stroud
Gloucestershire, GL5 4EP

www.amberley-books.com

British Library Cataloguing in Publication Data.
A catalogue record for this book is available from the British Library.

ISBN 978 1 4456 1009 2

Typeset in 10pt on 12pt Sabon.
Typesetting and Origination by Amberley Publishing.
Printed in the UK.

Contents

Gradwell with an enthusiasts' special train about to depart from Grimsargh station on 1 June 1957. (Courtesy N. Evans)

Barclay No. 2 and the unique D1 Stroudley 0-4-2 outisde the engine shed at Whittingham. (HCC/RMC).

Introduction

Preston is especially famous for its Guild Merchant conferred by ancient charter, drawn up by the town's burgesses in 1179, to implement the trading and mercantile sections of the charters. 'The Guild Merchant' originally allowed time for the town's burgesses to confirm their rights, revise statutes and to register their sons on the guild rolls, a legal function known as the 'Orders of the Guild'. Although the Guild had its origins during the reign of Henry II, the first documented Guild meeting is that of 1397, during the reign of King Richard II, though it was only after 1542, during the reign of King Henry VII, that the twenty-year cycle was adopted. The Guild of 1802 witnessed the rise of free trade and an altogether festival atmosphere which superseded the less formal proceedings of the past when the burgesses held the monopoly of the town's trade. The sequence of Preston Guilds every twenty years has only been interrupted once in 1942 when the Guild was cancelled because of wartime hostilities.

Preston Guild is nowadays the city's greatest indoor and outdoor extravaganza, culminating in a Saturday night torchlight procession and varied entertainment to suit all tastes. Previous Guilds have attracted half a million visitors from all Britain, including those Prestonians who revisit Preston (a city since 2002) from all over the world, eager to join in with the celebrations.

Welcome to the Preston Guild Special! In commemoration of Preston Guild 2012, we take a journey into history to explore the social, cultural and economic background to Preston during the Industrial Revolution, to see if they really lived up to the affectionate claim to be the 'good old days'. Paradoxically at a time of social unrest and economic strife certain of the populous were able to brighten up their day with the popular adage 'let's all go to the music hall'. The development of the Victorian Music Hall is certainly an important aspect of nineteenth-century social history and the Preston model broadly correlates with national trends insofar as Preston's mid-nineteenth-century pub singing saloons transposed to three major variety theatres built between 1905 and 1913, towards the end of the national music hall boom.

Retrospectively, star billing is at this juncture given to the former Whittingham Hospital Railway (WHR) that was opened in June 1889 and operated by Lancashire County Council. I grew up with this particular branch line and a host of memories have stimulated research. The Whittingham line was thought to be the only free

Above and below: The trade procession proceeds along Friargate, Preston, during Preston Guild 1972. (David Hindle)

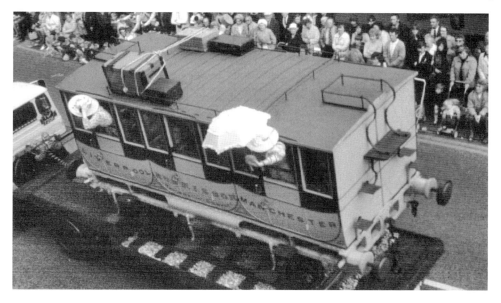

A Preston Guild 1972 re-enactment reminiscent of the Whittingham line during the Victorian and Edwardian eras. (David Hindle)

passenger railway in the world. Affectionately dubbed 'the nurses' special', it was primarily intended for hospital staff working shifts who resided in Preston and Ribbleton as well as the surrounding villages of Grimsargh, Longridge, Chipping and Ribchester but anyone else could travel entirely free of charge as many times as they could endure. For almost seventy years the general public rode on the 'no fare train' to and from Whittingham and maybe watched Christmas pantomimes staged in the ballroom, or enjoyed spending a summer's evening walking round the lake, whilst having a chat with the friendly patients and staff.

Before the piecemeal development of Whittingham Hospital in 1873, Charles Dickens visited Preston at the beginning of the infamous cotton famine in 1861 and is thought to have gained inspiration for his novel, *Hard Times*. As usual Dickens's literary eye was focused on 'the underdog' and the squalor and social deprivation that they had to endure. Appalling conditions endured by certain of the populace led to prostitution, pauperism and ill health and the need for the penniless and mentally ill to be fully institutionalised in the wretched workhouse or the new asylums such as Whittingham, which was served by its own private railway. Sadly, in euphemistic terms many patients gained a one way ticket to Whittingham and would never return to the outside world. Although the asylum was definitely no laughing matter, primary and anecdotal evidence suggests that the Whittingham Hospital line and its motley assortment of four locomotives and rolling stock was regarded in some quarters as yet another music hall joke! Indeed had it been able to grace the music hall stage it would probably have been regarded as a star 'novelty act' for it ranked as one of the most unique anachronistic Victorian steam railways in the country and even achieved international status. The WHR was precisely one mile, four furlongs and 9.7 chains

The Whittingham Hospital Railway, featuring Sentinel 0-4-0 *Gradwell* and D1 Stroudley *James Fryars* in the station yard. Beyond is the passenger stock alongside Whittingham Station. (Hospital Archives)

long (in period nomenclature) and was constructed to convey coal and provisions to the new hospital from the joint London & North Western and Lancashire & Yorkshire Preston to Longridge branch line at Grimsargh, and to get a clearer understanding of the former we commence with a chapter on the integrated Preston to Longridge railway (PLR).

By the mid-1950s the *raison d'être* of the Whittingham Hospital Railway was past and the very last passenger train along the line ran from Grimsargh to Whittingham on 29 June 1957. Shortly thereafter the track was lifted to remain as a scar on the landscape and legacy to the hospital and its Victorian steam railway. The tranquil railway scene between Grimsargh and Whittingham preserved the rustic essence and magnetism of this unique and historic line, which was inextricably linked into a pattern of rural life and a pastoral countryside that was a haven for local wildlife, symbolic of a bygone rural community. Without doubt the Whittingham line was a most unusual railway with many a tale to tell, thus firing the imagination of the author, who once worked at Whittingham and rode on the train. The charm of rural branch lines once epitomised those wonderful days of steam and all of the foregoing has provided the stimulus to share a measure of Lancashire's fascinating social and railway history.

CHAPTER ONE

'Grimsargh, change here for Whittingham Junction'

During the 1920s little Margaret Finch of Grimsargh inserted the princely sum of one penny into a Nestlé Chocolate dispenser on Grimsargh Railway Station platform, before catching the Longridge branch line passenger train into Preston to see a performance of J. M. Barrie's *Peter Pan* played at the old Empire Theatre on Church Street. The first railways provided new horizons for all classes of people who enjoyed the coming of the first music halls and theatres.

A ninety-six-year-old long retired nurse at Whittingham was a regular passenger on both the Whittingham and Longridge lines. The venerable gentleman described to me how in LMS days the trains from Preston and Deepdale were crowded with nurses who had to change at Grimsargh, where the porter hailed the passengers with the words 'Grimsargh, change here for Whittingham Junction'. In order to consider the origins of the Whittingham Hospital Railway, it is relevant to include a history of the integrated Preston to Longridge branch line that was first inspired in 1837.

The Preston to Longridge Railway Company – from Equine Quadruped to Iron Horse

Preston's place as a forerunner of national railway growth coincided with the opening of this combined mineral and passenger line, for it was on 1 May 1840 that the expanding Lancashire cotton town came to be linked with the village of Longridge, six and a half miles to the north-east. Following the arrival of the North Union Railway in 1838, the Preston to Longridge branch line was, chronologically, only the second railway to open in the Preston area and, in fact, just preceded even the Lancaster & Preston Junction Railway that was to evolve into the main Anglo-Scottish route. The line began in the ownership of the Preston to Longridge Railway Company (PLR) and was first conceived in 1835 as a means of conveying large blocks of Ashlar stone quarried from the Longridge quarries. Ashlar stone from Longridge was used in the construction of Preston's Harris Museum and Art Gallery and several other important buildings that transformed the interface of the town during the Victorian era.

The Chairman of the newly formed PLR, Thomas Batty Addison, stipulated that the railway would be horse-worked until the full working potential could be ascertained and then steam traction would be considered; eight years before the age of steam, genuine equine 'horse-power' was the means of propulsion up the steeply graded route. The quarries at Longridge were situated about four hundred feet above sea level and the railway company exploited the natural contours of the land by using gravity for part of the return journey. The beasts of burden even gained a complimentary return ticket, before boarding their own special carriage to be conveyed back down the steep gradients to Grimsargh and beyond. The horses would then regain their place at the head of the train and haul the heavy loads on to Preston before commencing the return journey.

The original Preston terminus of the branch was situated at Deepdale, near to the former coal sidings on Fletcher Road and was completely detached from Preston Station and the emerging rail network. The only intermediate station served the tiny village of Grimsargh and, perhaps surprisingly, utilised the west side of the Plough Inn as a booking office with adjacent platform. Indeed people who rode into Grimsargh to continue their journey by train began to discover that there was life beyond the village and they could now reach Preston on the iron horse by stabling the equine version at the Plough stables. The earliest station at Longridge was decidedly crude and was situated next to the main street and level crossing at Burey Lane – later called Berry Lane – in what was then a small village. Indeed, before Longridge Station was built in 1872 as an adjunct to the extant Towneley Arms Hotel, which was at first owned by the railway and opened in 1869, only rudimentary platform facilities were provided.[1] It was only after the railway was converted to steam power in 1848 and the industrial revolution had made its impact, that a rapid expansion of Longridge was triggered. A passenger service of sorts ran between Preston and Longridge on Sundays, Wednesdays and Saturdays with two trains a day from Preston at 7.30 a.m. and 4 p.m. returning from Longridge at 8.30 a.m. and 5 p.m. respectively. The fare from Preston to the Plough Inn at Grimsargh was 4d, and to Longridge was 6d.

The Line that Never Was

In 1846 the Preston to Longridge Railway was leased to a new consortium, the Fleetwood, Preston and West Riding Junction Railway Company (FPWRJRC), which formed an alliance with the PLR Company to rent and operate the railway. In June 1848, it was 'all change' to steam traction and the horses were pensioned off in the wake of this new technology and enjoyed a well-earned retirement in the tranquil fields of their home station at Grimsargh. Celebrations were held at Deepdale to mark the departure of the first steam locomotive to Longridge on Whit Monday, 1848. Officials of the railway company and a large party of officers from Fulwood Barracks were hauled by the engine *Addison* along with some 200 invited guests and a band of the 89th Regiment to the Longridge terminus. Various young ladies with their delighted partners tripped it lightly to the astonishment of villagers. The company had ambitious plans to promote the commercial viability of the port of Fleetwood with the profitable traffic of a new railway linking Fleetwood with the cities of Leeds and Hull by utilising a section of the PLR between Preston and Grimsargh. The company opened a one-mile extension to the detached line at Deepdale to link it with the railway network at Preston in 1850.

However, through the determined opposition of Lancashire landowners the Bill put forward by the FPWRJR was thrown out in the House of Lords. The company had spent an immense sum in making a tunnel through the town of Preston to connect their railway with the Fleetwood line and indeed the railway network. At Hurst Green – near Clitheroe – a railway cutting of over 200 metres in length survives as a monument to this ill-fated Victorian enterprise (Grid reference SD 682369). Nestling in splendid isolation the cutting is clearly recognisable as a detached section of that once ambitious project born of railway mania.

The abandoned project to extend the railway through the Ribble valley was described by Dobson (1877).

> This was a huge unfinished embankment. Climbing it we saw for some distance an excavation, with level bottom and sloping sides, continuing to the next dingle there was again the beginning of an embankment, as if to cross over the valley through which runs Clough Brook. I soon saw that this was a detached and uncompleted portion of that once ambitious project, the Fleetwood, Preston, and West Riding Junction railway. The Act for making this railway was passed in the year 1846. It was to utilise the Preston and Longridge and leave that line below Grimsargh, and pass by Hothersall, Dutton, Hurst Green, and Mitton to Whalley and into Yorkshire.

By 1851, the company's finances were in a dire state, showing a meagre profit of £924. Despite a more regularised passenger service, the impact of the aborted plans to reach West Yorkshire had drained financial resources. The Preston to Longridge Railway Company repossessed the line in 1852, following liquidation of the FPWRJR. However, after being moribund for four years, a newly reformed FPWRJR purchased the railway outright in 1856. At this time the line served the expanding village of Longridge with the Preston terminus at Maudland Bridge, and with intermediate stations at Deepdale Bridge, Ribbleton and Grimsargh. The extant Ribbleton Station first opened in 1854 and was curiously named Gammer Lane (Gamull Lane) then successively renamed Fulwood in 1856, when a bridge was built to carry Gamull Lane over the railway, and finally Ribbleton in 1900. In 1867 the FPWRJR Company lost its identity to the combined LYR/LNWR Company and a new station was built at Grimsargh in 1870, replacing the Plough Inn halt, which now had more space for serious drinkers. The joint-owned station at Grimsargh was a single-storey granite construction with a single platform situated on the south side of Long Site Lane adjacent to a level crossing.

With the opening of the Whittingham Hospital Railway (WHR) in 1889 a private railway station was built to serve the new railway at Grimsargh which had connecting facilities with the PLR. Grimsargh's second railway station was situated on the north side of the level crossing gates at Long Site Lane and thus Grimsargh became a railway junction. At the joint line station the porter now greeted his trains with 'Grimsargh, change here for Whittingham Junction'.

The Rise and Fall of the Preston to Longridge Branch Line

Naturally the WHR boosted freight and passenger traffic on the PLR. Conversely the Longridge branch was an essential feeder to the Whittingham line. Both lines probably reached their social and economic heyday during the first two decades of the twentieth century before a downward spiral was set to close both lines. During those halcyon days of the 'roaring twenties' there was the daily excitement of the Grimsargh level crossing gates being opened several times a day and the sight of the stationmaster emerging from his office to welcome passengers. They say 'all good things come to an end' and this was to include the Longridge branch. In the late 1920s the first omnibuses operated by the Pilot, Majestic and Claremont Bus companies from Clitheroe and Preston were on track to eclipse the passenger trains. The line was scheduled to close on Monday 2 June 1930, but in the absence of a Sunday service the last train from Longridge was at 10 p.m. on Saturday 31 May 1930.

As always there was more than a tinge of sadness at the time of closure and a column in the local newspaper evoked those feelings:

> The last journey on the Longridge line sharply contrasted with the aloof austerity of Preston and the warm feeling which the villagers showed as the train passed them for the last time. It was as well that someone should have remembered for there was nothing at Preston to indicate that ex-LYR Aspinall 2-4-2T No. 10646 was to make the last passenger journey on the ninety-year-old line. Driver Billington aptly summed up his last journey: 'Use is second nature and people get to know each other, that is why they are sorry.'

What the railways did to canal transport was now happening to this particular branch line and it was no longer wanted. The service which was begun with the hope of linking Lancashire with Yorkshire on 1 May 1840 never got beyond the seven miles to Longridge and now even that distance was seven miles too long. Following the withdrawal of passenger trains on the PLR, Whittingham passenger trains were timed to connect with bus services at Grimsargh. Freight and parcel traffic continued to operate from both Longridge and Grimsargh LMS Stations, thought it was the building of Courtaulds Factory in the 1930s that provided a lifeline for freight services on the PLR. Courtaulds' own industrial steam engines now hauled coal wagons along its own private railway to newly constructed interchange sidings adjacent to the Longridge line.

The Whittingham Hospital Railway closed to all traffic on 29 June 1957; its passenger services having survived those on the 'main-line' by all of twenty-seven years. However, its loss was to impact on the Longridge freight line, for during the months leading up to closure of the Whittingham branch, the PLR was still supplying

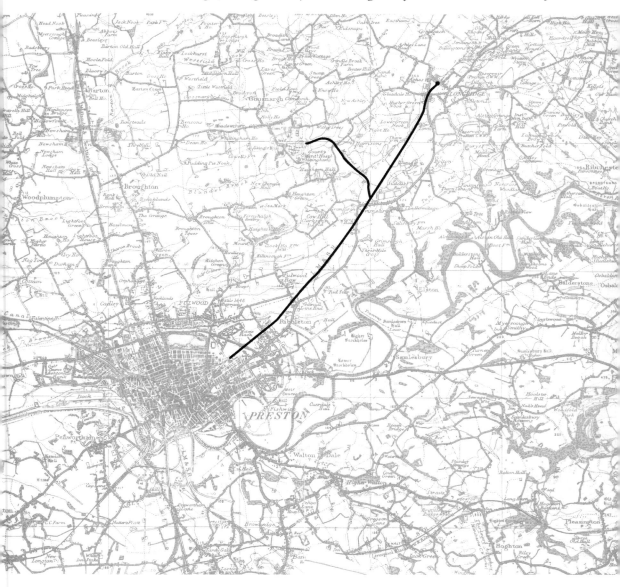

Ordnance Survey Map of 1924 showing the Preston to Longridge branch line. Principal stations were situated at Deepdale, Ribbleton, Grimsargh and Longridge. The Whittingham Hospital Railway is shown here as a mineral line veering off to the north-west from Whittingham Junction at Grimsargh. (Courtesy of Lancashire County Council)

Grimsargh station on the Longridge branch was built in 1870 next to the level crossing gates and just across the road from the Whittingham line. (Tom Heginbotham collection)

An unidentified LYR Aspinall heads past the Ministry of Supply building at Cromwell Road with a train for Grimsargh and Longridge in the 1950s. The veteran locomotives operating on the Longridge branch were not nearly so primitive as the engines on the WHR. (George Whiteman collection)

Austerity No. 90675 ready to depart from Longridge Station with the daily goods train to Preston *c.* 1964. (Courtesy of Alan Castle)

PRESTON & LONGRIDGE
RAILWAY.

List of Passenger Fares from the undermentioned Stations:--

FROM	TO	SINGLE JOURNEY TICKETS.			RETURN TICKETS.		
		First Class.	Second Class.	Gov. Class.	First Class.	Second Class.	Gov. Class
		s. d.	s. d.	s. d.	s. d.	s. d.	s. d.
PRESTON (Fishergate Station)	DEEPDALE ..	0 4	0 3	0 1½			
	FULWOOD ...	0 8	0 5	0 3			
	GRIMSARGH ..	0 11	0 7	0 5	1 6	1 0	0 8
	LONGRIDGE ..	1 3	0 11	0 7	2 0	1 6	1 0
DEEPDALE	PRESTON (Fishergate)	0 4	0 3	0 1½			
	FULWOOD ...	0 4	0 3	0 1½			
	GRIMSARGH ..	0 9	0 6	0 3½	1 3	0 10	0 6
	LONGRIDGE ..	1 0	0 9	0 5½	1 8	1 3	0 10
FULWOOD	PRESTON (Fishergate)	0 8	0 5	0 3			
	DEEPDALE ..	0 4	0 3	0 1½			
	GRIMSARGH ..	0 4	0 3	0 1½			
	LONGRIDGE ..	0 8	0 6	0 4			
GRIMSARGH	PRESTON (Fishergate)	0 11	0 7	0 5	1 6	1 0	0 8
	DEEPDALE ..	0 9	0 6	0 3½	1 3	0 10	0 6
	FULWOOD ...	0 4	0 3	0 1½			
	LONGRIDGE ..	0 6	0 4	0 2			
LONGRIDGE	PRESTON (Fishergate)	1 3	0 11	0 7	2 0	1 6	1 0
	DEEPDALE ..	1 0	0 9	0 5½	1 8	1 3	0 10
	FULWOOD ...	0 8	0 6	0 4			
	GRIMSARGH ..	0 6	0 4	0 2			

June 1st, 1885.

T. H. CARR,
Secretary.

A list of late Victorian era fares on the Preston to Longridge branch line showing the principal stations. (Author's collection)

coal to service the hospital's boilers. The decline of the textile and cottage industries and cessation of quarrying at Longridge saw the last freight train traverse the track from Courtaulds Factory to Longridge during November 1967. However, it was the demolition of the landmark Courtaulds' chimneys in 1980 that signalled the end of the last substantial section of the Longridge branch line from Deepdale Junction to Courtaulds' exchange sidings. Thus during the second half of the twentieth century, there were three phased closures of the branch line. The first freight cutback was from Longridge to Courtaulds Factory in 1967. The next section to close was from Courtaulds to Deepdale junction in 1980, culminating in the closure of the final triangular stretch of track between Maudland Junction and the coal distribution depot in Fletcher Road, Deepdale in 1994. Today only a small stretch of long-abandoned track exists from Maudland to Skeffington Road, marking the final chapter of the Longridge line.

The Plough Inn at the hub of Grimsargh village. The aerial photograph shows to the top left the cleared site of the former WHR station, awaiting development. The railway line transformed the historic bowling green from a round to an oval one when the railway was first constructed in 1838–40. (Tom Heginbotham collection)

CHAPTER TWO

Preston During
the Industrial Revolution

Throughout the nineteenth and early twentieth centuries, Preston was crammed with mills, terraced houses and cobbled streets. This was at the height of the Industrial Revolution, when 'King Cotton' was supreme, though there were little prosperity for certain factions. Throughout the hard times endured in Victorian Preston, there were inebriates, destitute paupers and those branded mentally ill, including pregnant single women, many of whom were institutionalised for their own safety and well-being.

Houses were concentrated in the south-east and north-west areas of the town close to where the earliest spinning mills had been built. 'Preston was compact in area and any reasonably fit adult could walk anywhere in the town in under half an hour.'[2] Preston was the also the first provincial town to be lit by gas, as early as 1816, and this made for a safer environment when venturing into the town at night. In 1851 the total number of houses was 11,543 and each house had an average of almost six occupants. With this rapid growth had come the predictable sanitary and housing problems. Conditions were very cramped, frequently damp with poor hygiene standards, lighting and sanitation. Preston was without piped water, drains or sewers and the narrow passageway beyond the privy in the back yard was the place where the privy pails were emptied. Cholera and typhus were rampant and infant mortality was exceptionally high among working-class families.

During the first half of the nineteenth century Preston's population increased from 11,887 people in 1801 to 69,361 in 1851. Commensurate with the growth of the dominant textile industry the steadily rising population increased to 91.500 by 1881. Preston was at the forefront of automation when John Horrocks opened his first factory in 1790, closely followed by three more factories during the same decade. This was due in no small measure to one of Preston's most famous sons, Sir Richard Arkwright, born in 1732. He developed and patented a water frame based spinning machine that was to be a catalyst for the mechanisation of the industry throughout Britain; eventually superseding the domestic home industry. Thus Preston became one of the earliest and greatest centres of the Lancashire cotton industry and, owing to its commanding position in the centre of the county, became a chief centre of industrial relations. Up to 3,000 hand-loom weavers lived in the town in the 1830s with over a thousand houses built for them.

During 1851 the town's economy was still dominated by the textile industry, which continued into Edwardian times. Anderson's analysis of the 1851 census provides further evidence of the dominance of the textile industry as well as demographic considerations: 'The adult population over 20 years old comprised 32% of men and 28% of women engaged in cotton manufacture as well as a high percentage of children.. Most migrants came from within a radius of 15 to 20 miles … About a third of the population were artisans.'[3] The cotton industry reached its peak in the decade before the Great War employing 30,000 people before the onset of the industries decline by 1920.

Joseph Livesey was born in Walton-le-dale, Preston, and was a founding member of the Preston Temperance Society. Livesey and six others introduced teetotalism to the movement through their innovation of the total abstinence pledge at Preston's first Temperance Hall on 1 September 1832. It follows that the temperance movement was especially active in Preston, campaigning against drunkenness and low moral standards in Preston's growing number of public houses and singing saloons throughout much of the Victorian era.

As well as expressing their condemnation in the strongest persuasive terms, those who promoted temperance and respectability knew from the beginning that alternative entertainments and leisure persuits were needed if they were to win converts to their cause. Thus rational recreation was promulgated in Preston by an influential section of the town's middle-class leaders and temperance advocates. Indeed, from the mid-1840s the most important agency of rational recreation was the temperance movement. The rationale was to lure the working class away from leisure pursuits associated with alcohol consumption through respectable counter attractions, whereby the values of rational recreation might be internalised. Preston Corporation first enclosed 100 acres of Preston Moor as Moor Park as early as 1834. With further development of Miller and Moor parks in the early 1860s, the council aimed to provide recreational facilities and at the same time engage textile workers with employment in landscaping at the height of the cotton famine.

The Liberal members, with their alliance with the nonconformist and teetotal movement, welcomed any move to lure the workers away from the pub environment.[4] Education and self-improvement were another side to the promotion of respectability, an issue referred to by the Recorder of Preston, Joseph Catterall, in 1869 when he attacked the pub culture:

> There ought to be very stringent regulations as to prostitutes and persons of notoriously bad character being allowed to congregate together in these houses. Yet supposing that the best licensing system possible should be carried out, we should still be far from suppressing the vice of drunkenness and its too often criminal results. This can only be done by education, judiciously adapted to the wants of our populations.[5]

The Mechanics' Institute movement of the 1820s represented the first attempt to moralise the working classes by combining instruction on science and mechanics with lectures, libraries and amusement which would benefit their work. The first Mechanics' Institute opened in Preston in 1828 at No. 11 Cannon Street. It was

Top: 'The old Shambles' and the Shoulder of Mutton pub.
Above: The starch houses viewed from High Street (hence Starch-house Square), remembered by older Prestonians as the site of a bus station.

The watercolours of Edwin Beattie (1845–1917) were kindly provided by Mr Andrew Mather and are reproduced courtesy of the Jesuit Community at St Wilfrid's, Preston.

called the Preston Institute for the Diffusion of Knowledge. Its aims were to facilitate and promote the diffusion of knowledge among the operative mechanics and other inhabitants of Preston. The first officers of the Institute were all professional men and included Joseph Livesey, the founder of Temperance and one of the town's chief benefactors. The subscriptions were 6s 6d a year and this included access to a library of 1,500 books which circulated at the rate of 300 a week. During 1829 classes of chemistry and English grammar and composition were held. Among the members in 1841 there were eighty-five clerks and shop-men, seventy-six tradesmen, seventeen mechanics, thirty-four joiners and other operatives but only six factory hands. The first attempt to fund a new building was made in 1840.

The Institution's new building was known as the Aveham Institution and was opened in October 1849. The main storey had a large library, a reading room, committee rooms, and several classrooms. A theatre was attached to the institution, where entertainment and public meetings were held. Education was to be the key at the time of Dickens' mid-century visits to Preston and no doubt this would have the effect of lifting the souls of the impoverished cotton workers during the great lockout. However, as the Reverend John Clay, Chaplain to the House of Correction, said in 1852, 'The Avenham Institute, does not do the good one would wish it cannot rival the beer shops and public houses.'[6] Generally in Preston and elsewhere there were limitations on learning.

As the mills and factories grew, so did the churches and chapels. With the expansion of Preston around 1852 many new churches were built. For those seeking spiritual guidance the church may have provided a safe haven and perhaps acted as a diversion from the poverty they endured. The Methodists, inspired by John Wesley, who preached four times in the town, had their Wesleyan chapel in Lune Street built in 1817. Nonconformists included Baptists, Quakers, and Unitarians. Though not all Preston nonconformists supported teetotalism, the prominent early teetotallers all came from the Liberal/Radical nonconformist section of society, and were backed by the Whig *Preston Chronicle* against the Tory *Preston Pilot*.[7] Many temperance reformers, especially nonconformists were suspicious of theatres, dancing and Sunday secular enjoyments. 'We presume that nearly all our readers are opposed to the theatre, wrote the *Weekly Record*, a leading temperance paper on 8 November, 1862.'

The Roman Catholic population grew, bolstered by large numbers of Irish people settling in Preston from 1840. Clemet concluded that half the population of Preston was Church of England, a third Roman Catholic and the rest Nonconformist. 'The Politics of Churchmen in Preston are consequently of a Conservative or Tory type.'[8] Although the liberals were not very successful in obtaining the Catholic and non-conformist vote, secular mixing between the classes was fostered by the parish tea and concert parties and peaked in the late Victorian era. Sunday Schools were intended to deflect children from the streets, pubs and music halls, offering religion through education, organised picnics and railway excursions. 'In 1851 the index of church attendance for Preston was only about half of that of other cotton towns.'[9]

The 1851 Census of Religious Worship in Preston

Places of Worship and Religious denomination	Total	Total No of attendants Sunday morning 30 March 1851
Total No. Churches	29	11803
Church of England	10	2479
Independents	2	1065
Particular Baptists	2	437
Scotch Baptists	1	23
Society of Friends	1	153
Unitarians	1	86
Wesleyan Methodists	3	1505
Primitive Methodists	1	342
Wesleyan Association	1	254
Huntingdon's Conner	1	142
New Church	1	100
Isolated Congregations	1	120
Roman Catholics	4	5097

Preston was, until 1945, a two-seat constituency, one of the last constituencies to return two MPs. From the early days of the nineteenth century up to the 1830s the returns had been equally divided between Whigs and Tories. After 1840 the balance tipped towards the Liberals but again became more equally divided between Liberal and Tory from 1852–59. In 1874, the great majority of the town's working class voted for the two Tory candidates. Edward Hermon, the greatest textile employer in the town received a massive 6,512 votes.[10] Joyce states that 'the Conservative party's electoral success owed much to its involvement with the drink trade and that the association between temperance and liberalism was close.'[11] Working class support for the Tory candidate may therefore indicate some support the status quo and that the employer had greater awareness of working class values and interests. During the 1860s the two Preston seats were secured by Conservatives, who held them from 1859 until 1906.[12] It was not until 1906 that Preston gained its first Labour MP following the formation of the Independent Labour Party in 1893.

Widespread improvement of the Lancashire economy followed a wages boom in the early 1870s with improved housing, municipal amenities and a reduction of disease and premature death. During 1877 the Chief Constable of Preston reflected on the level of increased prosperity of textile workers: 'They earn pretty fair wages and as a rule they spend pretty freely. A man receives his wages on a Friday and generally he will spend a portion of those in drink before he gets home.'

In Preston, extensive improvements and slum clearance programmes were introduced by the Bye Laws of 1876 and the Preston Improvement Act 1880. Morgan confirms that Preston's housing was revolutionised with new housing good enough to survive until the present day.

The nineteenth-century journalist and historian Anthony Hewitson refers to the very real advances made by the time of the Preston Guild (1882) in the social and physical fabric of the town. The Albert Edward Dock opened for commercial trading on 25 June 1892, immediately following the official opening ceremony, performed by Prince Albert, the Duke of Edinburgh, and the second son of Queen Victoria.

In 1897 Dick Kerr established his engineering works on a large site on Strand Road to meet the growing demand for tramcars and railway locomotives. Engineering was an important industry in the town, employing over ten per cent of the male workers of the town, as against twenty-three per cent in all branches of cotton.[13] The first railways acted as a catalyst for economic growth and transformed the social and economic prosperity of the country's towns and villages. At the end of the Victorian era the social climate and economy of Preston had progressed with less overcrowding, the proliferation of new industries, higher wages and an improved standard of living for a population of 112,989 by 1901.

The Victorian historian and journalist Anthony Hewitson, writing in 1883, did not speak too favourably about the original North Union Station or of the first steam engines: 'At Preston the station was one of the most dismal, dilapidated, disgraceful-looking structures in Christendom. It was not only a very ill-looking, but an exceedingly inconvenient dangerous station ... Often, when a heavy train was leaving Preston for the north, porters had to push at the side by way of giving them

The very last hoot of the old TSS *Manxman* alongside her berth at Preston Dock on 3 October 1982. The Albert Edward Dock was officially opened in 1892 but ceased to operate as a commercial trading port in 1981. (Courtesy of Peter Fitton)

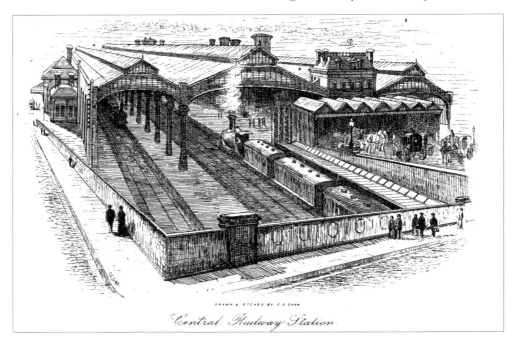

The Victorian Central Railway Station, Preston. (Hewitson, *A History of Preston*, 1883)

How Preston Railway Station looked on 23 August 1972, at the time of the electrification of the West Coast Main Line. (Courtesy of Peter Fitton)

A rare photograph of the experimental turbo-locomotive 765GT3 on a down train at Preston station on 20 October 1961. (Tony Gillett)

Jubilee Class No. 45592 *Indore* makes a brisk start from Preston station, *c.* 1961. (Tony Gillett)

The year is 1961, the location the south end of Preston station. Three types of motive power are depicted above: (left) English Electric Type 4 diesel No. D 310; (centre) Craven DMU; Stanier Class 5 No. 44776. (Tony Gillett)

The commanding spire of St Walburgh's church, Preston, here complements the railway scene with Stanier Class 5 No. 45077 and Standard Class No. 73046 on an up train from Blackpool *c.* 1961, double heading. (Tony Gillett)

assistance' – sounds like just another music hall joke, in fact. Railway beginnings in Preston (and nationally) coincide with the emergence of singing saloons, circus and music hall during the 1840/50s, laying the foundations of the entertainment and travel industries. The original Preston Station of 1838 was the earliest within the bounds of the present county of Lancashire. Originally Preston Station comprised only two platforms, which had expanded to six tracks, four platforms and an extended station building by 1847. Increased volume of traffic and the appalling lack of facilities on the original station led to the construction of a more substantial structure, which was completed by the firm of Cooper and Tullis in July 1880. Further extensions were made in 1903 and 1913, when Preston Station reached its zenith with a total of fifteen platforms inclusive of bays.

Coronation Pacific No. 46239 *City of Chester* heads the down Royal Scot through Preston station *c.* 1961. (Tony Gillett)

CHAPTER THREE

A One-way Ticket to Whittingham Hospital

Ladies and Gentlemen,

And now for your sincere unmitigated enjoyment and delight I have much pleasure in presenting tonight's star turn – an anthology of authentic events and an anecdotal compendium verifiable with a photographic portfolio of the indefatigable antediluvian iron horse that toiled between the stations of Grimsargh and Whittingham in the County of Lancashire and whose memory is now to be preserved for posterity, the renowned and anachronistic 'Whittingham Hospital Railway'. At the end of the show even Queen Victoria might be amused, I think!

The idealist interpretation is that the 'Good Old Days' is seen as romanticised expression of authentic working class culture, but with or without the music hall were they really the 'Good Old Days'? This chapter examines some of the possible causes of poor mental health, pauperism and destitution during the Industrial Revolution that led to the building of the Victorian asylums. Whittingham's patients came from a wide catchment area, though central Lancashire was served by neighbouring hospitals at Calderstones, Brockhall, Langho, Rainhill, Lancaster and other such institutions scattered throughout north-west England.

We begin with 'the demon drink'. The Beer Shop Act of 1830 exacerbated the local drink problem, when it brought about 190 beer houses to Preston between 1830 and 1834 and fuelled the temperance cause with which the movement coincided. As industry and population boomed so did the number of public houses, especially in the first half of the nineteenth century. During 1868, the number of drink places per person in Preston reached a peak and was higher than the national average, with a total of around 490 licensed premises.

Beer shops or houses were judged to be a haven for thieves and prostitutes and their overall tone stimulated newspaper correspondents and reformers to vigorously attack the subculture in the local press:

In another beer-house, fiddling and singing is the order of the night; in every one it is vice with the paint off, for most, if not all, of the men, are thieves or worse, and the women, without exception, are prostitutes of the lowest and most depraved class. Here they are unmistakeably plying their horrid vocation, drinking almost fiercely. Cards and dominoes appear to be great favourites, but it does not appear that they are gambling, perhaps because they have nothing to gamble for.

With the considerable expansion of the railway network Preston soon became an important railway junction that was commensurate with the so called 'good old days' of the Victorian music hall and legitimate theatre. Remarkably, such great exponents of culture as Franz Liszt, Niccolo Paganini, Oscar Wilde and Sir Henry Irving delighted audiences during the nineteenth century at Preston's illustrious Theatre Royal on Fishergate, which opened as early as 1802.

The great Hungarian-born composer and performer Franz Liszt graced the stage of the Theatre Royal, Preston on Wednesday 2 December 1840. As part of the same tour Liszt also played at five North West venues, in Halifax, Liverpool, Manchester, Rochdale and Preston. By contrast, however, the hoi polloi including young children frequented less glamorous establishments, which were in fact embryonic music halls in dubious beer houses and singing saloons: 'In one low dirty room of a beer-house crowded with young men and low prostitutes, a fiddler is scraping away at an old fiddle and a girl is step dancing.' This sort of activity can be identified as the genre of 'free and easies', the first phase of music hall development. The girl's step dancing represents a link with a local tradition in the cotton mills, where a large workforce of women would start beating out a rhythm with their wooden clogs in time to the shuttles buzzing back and forth on the loom. Step-dancing or 'Lancashire Clog', became a favourite with mill-workers in Preston and was performed extensively in music hall while representing a strong northern culture and perhaps even solidarity and local pride during Preston's Industrial Revolution.

An alarmingly high number Preston's young people frequented the pub music halls, also known as singing saloons or concert halls, which superseded the impromptu free and easy gigs. During January 1865, the *Chronicle* reported on the Black Swan Concert Hall situated on Water Street, Preston; here the basic accommodation consisted of a 'concert hall measuring 20' x 16', cheap decorations, a little stage and rough wooden seats occupied by 60 or 70 lads and lassies of the cotton operative class. Young girls gaudily dressed were seated supping porter which they had exchanged for a refreshment ticket.'

During the early years of music hall, the two names 'music hall' and 'variety' were used interchangeably, though the generic music hall always had a Chairman, and here the entertainment was often ancillary to the sale and consumption of intoxicating liquor. At Preston's established concert halls, which were annexed to public houses, the venerable Chairman introduced clog dancers, musicians, ballad and operatic singers, jugglers, ventriloquists, clowns, serio-comic and circus inspired novelty acts (see below).

Venue and Date	Programme	Remarks
King's Head The Era, 28. 1. 72	Professor Capron – ventriloquist, F. Raymond – impersonator and clog dancer, The Brothers Panell – French clowns with performing dogs, Miss Amy Turner and Miss B. Anderson – serio-comic, Miss Jessie Danvers – vocalist and clog dancer, Tom Melbourne – star comic.	Clog dancers typical music hall genre in Preston.
George Concert Hall, Friargate. The Era 21. 7. 1878	Tom and Rose Merry, (duettists, vocalists and dancers), Marie Santley (serio-comic), Will Atkins (comic), Mr and Mrs Patrick Miles and Young Ireland (known as the solid man) and Tom Walker described as topical.	Preston's established pub concert hall of 1864.

Although historians search for the identity of the very first English music hall, its identity is a bit like the search for the Holy Grail. The establishment of a purpose-built concert room or music hall first came to Preston with the opening of the Albion in 1839, which places Preston at the forefront of national music hall growth, with a concert room capable of accommodating up to six hundred people. Prison Chaplain the Reverend John Clay provides evidence of three extant early Preston concert halls in his 1842 Annual Report: 'One of the concert rooms, capable of holding 650 persons was opened in the summer of 1839. Two others of smaller dimension were opened in the spring of 1841.' Therefore a pattern of growth and evidence of commercialisation and regularity of the industry begins to emerge, notwithstanding the growth of the music hall industry.

The Lancashire 'Cotton Famine' (1861–64) brought mass unemployment and poverty to Preston and extensive areas of Lancashire at the time of the American Civil War (1861–65.) Charles Dickens showed empathy to the workforce when he addressed the cotton workers of the town in 1861 and gave readings from *A Christmas Carol* and *The Pickwick Papers*, at the Corn Exchange, but with seats ranging from 1s to 4s the town was hardly living up to 'great expectations'. Historians have debated the extent to which the depression was caused by the North's blockade of southern shipping or whether the war masked an impending cyclical trade depression; a commercial crisis on this scale had profound economic and social implications for Preston, particularly as many of the working class were, in effect, reduced to pauperism.

Below the surface there was still plenty to shock in the immediate post-famine period with miscreants, prostitutes and vagrants indulging in both petty and serious crime. Prostitution was rife on the streets of Preston in the mid- to late Victorian era and they also used music halls for business. Here middle class men could meet working class women, often prostitutes:

Is it not possible for a man to walk the distance between the Parish Church and the Theatre Royal, without being accosted and stopped by numbers of girls many of them of an age in which, in ordinary life a girl is considered a child. The area of the Orchard and Friargate is infested by bonnet-less young girls ... Something ought to be done about the 120 women and girls known to the police as being on the streets of Preston ... there are scores of children on the streets of Preston.

Indeed the conditions in Victorian Preston were deplorable during the 1860s. Judging by reports from 1865 in the *Preston Chronicle*, had Charles Dickens visited the local thief's kitchen he would probably have encountered the Preston equivalent of Oliver Twist:

Congregations of all sorts of men, women and children are gathered in the thief's kitchen. In all of them there are scales with which the proprietor weighs the bread begged by the tramps during the day, before he purchases it. In these places lads, women, men, girls, beggars, thieves, tramps, vagabonds, cripples and prostitutes sleep together, without any respect to age or any distinction of sex, huddling in imperfectly ventilated rooms, and taking off their clothing before retiring to rest on account of the vermin.[14]

The report concluded with the remark, 'As to the houses of ill fame, we have no new remedy to suggest. There were twenty-seven lodging houses of receivers of stolen goods, thirty-one public houses, twenty-five beer houses, two coffee shops, and six suspected houses all of which are known resorts of thief's and prostitutes and sixty one brothels.'

The genre of early music hall in Preston came under pressure not only because of its working-class origins but also because of its close links with the drinks trade, both of which were factors in its presumed lack of respectability, if not outright immorality. Furthermore, evidence from 1865 illustrates the level of extreme poverty, deprivation and vulnerability of young people:

The singing room we visited was up a flight of steps out of a stable yard, in a court not a hundred miles from the market place ... Can any good emanate from such places ... Little by little the girl loses her modesty, and the end is as sure and certain as is the clergyman's hope of her joyful resurrection after her life of vice with its daily battling with hunger, and her wretched death in the workhouse infirmary.[15]

The social reformer Joseph Livesey campaigned against the Poor Law and it is not surprising that Charles Dickens gained some insight for the Preston-based novel *Hard Times*, where his literary eye was focused on squalor and the appalling conditions which ultimately consigned certain of the populous to labour at the workhouse treadmill.

The prospect of incarceration in the one of the town's parish workhouses or in the single union workhouse in Watling Street Road first established in 1868 was a daunting one. In the above passage the girl's 'wretched death in the workhouse infirmary' epitomises tragic stories of sadness and misfortune that are sometimes told about workhouse inmates. In May 1864, the *Chronicle* emphasised the deterrent effect of the proposed new building. 'One large workhouse would have more of a deterrent effect than the honey-suckle fronted places we now have. It would be a bigger and more tremendous embodiment of pauperism – that repulsive idea that we associate with workhouses would be more tangible.' The evidence illustrates that the social conditions in mid-Victorian Preston could hardly have equated with the notion of the 'good old days', and clearly there was a need for the legislative process to take its course with regard to hospitalising paupers and the mentally ill.

The Regulation, Care and Treatment of Lunatics Act of 1845 required the provision of asylums for the care of pauper lunatics. Legislation in 1853 prohibited restraining devices on lunatics in workhouses, which led to pressure for the mentally ill to be fully institutionalised. At a time when facilities fell short of the demand for accommodation, it was decided to build a 1,000-bed asylum at Whittingham, based on a house that was renamed St Luke's, and work then commenced on the first of four main phases. During construction building materials were brought by road from Preston and Longridge. Bricks were made on-site; the source being what became an ornamental lake, one that is referred to on old maps as the 'fish pond'. It was not until 1873 that the first patients were admitted. St Luke's main building incorporated wards and a superb ballroom and, viewed from the front elevation, the building could easily have passed off as one of the stately homes of England.

An open day in the heyday of Whittingham. (Hospital Archives)

Ward scene at Whittingham Hospital at the beginning of the twentieth century. (Hospital Archives)

Generally, an 'open door principle' allowed patients access to over two acres of hospital park-like grounds incorporating gardens, a cricket pitch and an ornamental lake. (Hospital Archives)

In 1878 Cooper & Tullis built the St John's Annex at Whittingham and in 1884 an Infectious Diseases Sanatorium was established, known as Fryars' Villa, after Alderman James Fryar, who was Chairman of the Hospital Committee. Alderman Fryars was later (1948) to have a Whittingham Hospital railway engine named after him – a veteran Stroudley D1 0-4-2, renamed *James Fryars*, which originally hailed from the London, Brighton & South Coast Railway!

In 1890 the 'Lunacy Act' was passed by Parliament, giving the power to county authorities to build asylums, using money sourced from council rates. This was one of the greatest pieces of legislation in the history of Victorian asylums and led to improvements; for example by 1894 the grounds had been illuminated by a new invention – electric lamps. However, it was not until 1 April 1893 that the official opening of the hospital took place. Conditions at the asylum were stringent. Rules for staff were extremely harsh and like the patients, they too probably became institutionalised. The nurses had to be on duty at 6 a.m. and retire to bed at 10 p.m. Nurses were allowed out for only one weekday every three weeks and on one Sunday every month, at a time when public transport was virtually non-existent. An 'open door' principle for patients was eventually extended to the grounds and gardens as well as the local village of Goosnargh. Recreational and sporting prowess was encouraged and the hospital's own brass band attained high standards with its compositional elements of both patients and staff.

Whittingham's West Annex was constructed in 1912 to become known as St Margaret's division; prior to this, Cameron House was completed and named after James Cameron. St Margaret's officially opened in 1914, and by 1915 total patient capacity was recorded as being 2,820. The end of the Great War brought a change of name from Whittingham Asylum to Whittingham Mental Hospital and, by the outbreak of the Second World War; the patient population was 3,533, which made it the largest mental hospital in the country.

Long before the hospital's construction was finished, a permanently manned stud of horse-drawn carts was used to convey supplies from Preston or Longridge Railway Station to Whittingham Hospital. In 1884, a proposed 'Whittingham Tramway' was first being conceived as a vital link with the outside world, for it was not until 1884 that telephone communications were established between the remote hospital and Preston. A four-man committee was established at Whittingham, and it was estimated that the cost of the 2,863-yard standard-gauge line, at £12,000, would give an annual saving of £1,050 over road haulage. However, this was conditional upon the LNWR and LYR Joint Ownership working the service. The railway company declined, but instead granted junction facilities with their 'main line' at Grimsargh. On 1 October 1884, application was made for a siding to connect the proposed asylum railway to Grimsargh Station.[16]

There was considerable wrangling at the hospital between the finance and general purposes committee and its four-man sub-committee. Following protracted exchanges within the hospital's boardroom, it was beginning to look like the whole concept of a railway was about to be thwarted. As an aside there was even serious gossip that a certain comedian on the committee aired the view: 'Where is Grimsargh? I fear that this is potentially a line to nowhere. The problem with a line to nowhere is that our staff and patients will have no way of knowing when they have got there!'

Notwithstanding this completely unfounded rumour, further revision of the costs brought the estimated price down to £9,000 but the finance committee had still rejected the proposal. Undaunted, the sub-committee decided to circumvent internal dissension by applying the full might of the law and, in January, 1885, the Annual Sessions at Preston presented a bill to parliament, which was duly approved. Although the finance committee conceded, it is likely that the sub-committee made certain concessions.

The original sub-committee became known as the 'Tramway Sub Committee'. Due to strong opposition from landowners, a period of two years elapsed before all the necessary land could finally be purchased. Railway archives from 1887 describe: 'It was proposed to make a tramway. A plan of the junction has been prepared and it is proposed to carry out work, subject to county authorities paying the cost, and agreeing to pay the future expense and maintenance.'[17] The first sod was cut at Grimsargh in 1887, as a prelude to major constructional difficulties. The actual construction work was delayed by wet and cold weather across difficult terrain, the bad winter of 1887, for example, causing severe earth movements and the embankment near to Whittingham to slip. The bulk of the navvies who worked on construction of the first railways were casual employees and they would have evidently had to work particularly hard in constructing the Whittingham line. By 1888, the £9,000 allotted for the railway was almost spent. Application was then made to the Finance Committee for a further

'Grimsargh, change for Whittingham Junction.' The photograph shows Grimsargh (WHR) Station on 1 May 1954, with the British Railways station behind the semaphore signal. (Courtesy of Gordon Biddle)

Grimsargh station (PLR) and level crossing, *c.* 1961. (Tom Heginbotham collection)

The end of the platform at Grimsargh station (WHR) showing the run-round loop and the link with the PLR (right). (Courtesy of Gordon Biddle)

Empty coal wagons from Whittingham waiting to go back onto the Longridge branch at Grimsargh. Note even at this late stage (1 June 1957) the recent attention to the track and new ballast. (Courtesy of Dorron Harper)

Whittingham Station and weighbridge office where the line forked to the engine shed, sidings and the hospital grounds. (N. Evans collection)

£5,000 that was needed to complete the works and to provide a locomotive and rolling stock, thus avoiding any need for horse traction. Extra funding was provided and a Barclay 0-4-0 saddle-tank engine was purchased from Andrew Barclay & Sons, Kilmarnock, in 1888, together with minimal stock and, in March 1889, it was reported that the permanent way was finished.

Traffic commenced running on the line in June, 1889. The Victorian historian, Tom Smith, alluded to the forthcoming opening of the Whittingham branch:

> A tramway has just been completed between the Asylum and Grimsargh Station, on the Preston to Longridge railway line. We venture to hope that this tramway will, in a short time, be open to the people of Whittingham and Goosnargh, as in such a case the district will be largely developed … The steam tram to Whittingham Asylum starts from Grimsargh; but costly as the venture had proved to the county ratepayers, the line is not allowed to be utilised by the public for local traffic – a state of affairs which doubtless the County Council will at once rectify for local traffic.

The WHR probably had little impact on the village of Goosnargh, although the two railway stations at Grimsargh undoubtedly led to the expansion of Grimsargh. Furthermore, the line was used by the general public from the time of its opening.

CHAPTER FOUR

The Nurses' Special – a Music Hall Conundrum

We have seen that the Whittingham line was constructed between 1887/89 to convey coal and provisions to the new hospital, linking it with the joint London North Western and Lancashire and Yorkshire's Preston to Longridge branch line at Grimsargh. Passengers followed almost immediately on the WHR and private stations were built at either end of the almost two-mile-long standard-gauge line. The hospital was built in a rural locality about eight miles north-east of Preston, and about two miles from the cruciform village of Grimsargh (formerly Grimsargh with Brockholes). Grimsargh, like the nearby village of Goosnargh (adjacent to Whittingham Hospital), originates from a Norse settlement and agricultural manor.

Moreover, the WHR was originally built to solve a Victorian conundrum – how to connect a remote and rural hospital establishment with the outside world to solve the hospital's supply problems with coal and provisions. The answer to this enigma was to build a private railway and for almost seventy years a quaint and diminutive train slowly crossed over the level crossing in front of Whittingham St Luke's main hospital building, providing a somewhat surreal encounter for patients and visitors alike. Undoubtedly unique, it claimed to be the only free passenger railway in the world and overall its characteristics have been likened to a music hall joke.

Even before the dawn of railway preservation the line was well known to enthusiasts for its archaic locomotives and rolling stock. The railway's heritage was, somewhat surprisingly, even extended far beyond the shores of England. In fact, long before the days of the internet, the railway's inimitable characteristics were being acclaimed in San Francisco with the slogan, 'You can travel 50 miles a day for nothing on the Grimsargh–Whittingham line, England.'

However, it was rumoured in the States that a passenger had complained that the problem with a free railway was that it took all the fun out of going nowhere for 50 miles and finding an adder that could neither add nor subtract! (See page 42) On a more serious note, however, in 1919, consideration was given to charging passengers, but nevertheless the 'no fare train' prevailed throughout its entire existence. Indeed the tranquil railway scene between Grimsargh and Whittingham saw minimal change for almost seventy years. Thus who could resist boarding the train at Grimsargh's quaint branch line station for a free ride to Whittingham on this Victorian relic to discover its quirky features?

Amazingly, Barclay No. 1 and its period passenger stock achieved international celebrity status and was even billed in San Francisco, where it evidently appealed to curious Americans and devotees of railway history. This drawing of the Whittingham train appeared in the *San Francisco Examiner* on 27 September 1933. The caption read, 'No fare train. You can travel fifty miles a day for nothing on the Grimsargh to Whittingham line, England.' (Author's collection)

Features of the WHR and an encounter with a certain 'James Fryars'

The spotlight now turns to my own lasting impressions of a journey along the line around 1953, when Grandfather Bowman first introduced me to the delights of the Whittingham line. The memory of the quaint old engine in the bay at Grimsargh Station and the rattling and shaking of the wooden carriages trundling along the single track has stayed with me to this very day, even though for many fellow passengers it was just a functional train ride to work. I was fortunate to know Grimsargh in those halcyon days when the main Longsight Lane (now Preston Road) was obstructed twice a day by the level crossing gates. As a tired Aspinall ex-LYR 0-6-0 steam engine on the Longridge branch prepared to show its true colours in tackling the ascent

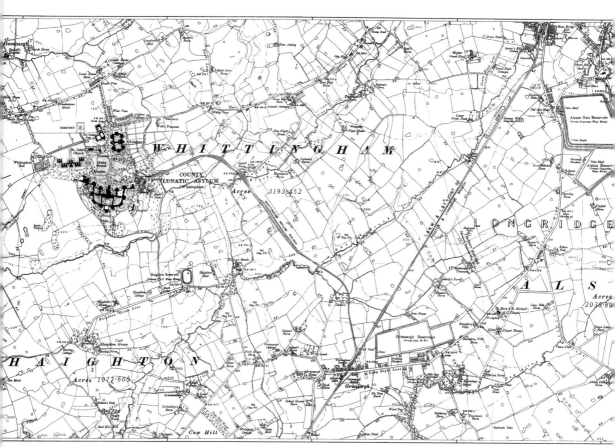

Ordnance Survey map of 1914 (then six inches to one mile), illustrating the Preston to Longridge railway and associated Whittingham Hospital branch. (Lancashire County Council)

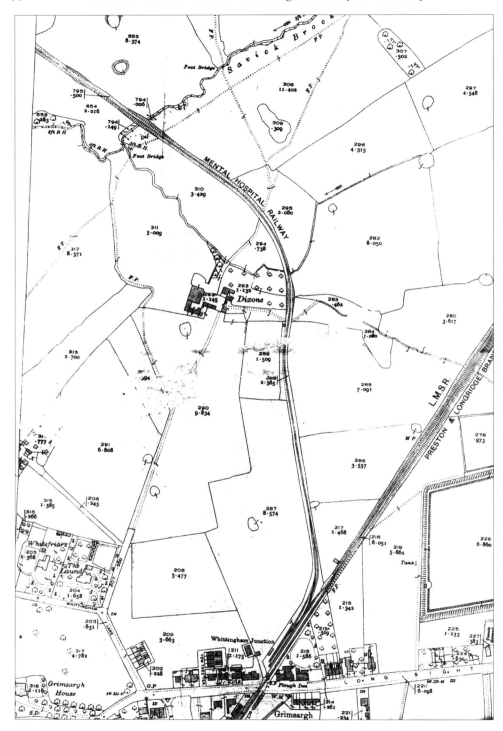

25-inch to one-mile Ordnance Survey map from 1938 showing the village of Grimsargh and the junction of the PLR with the WHR. Interestingly, the trailing junction linking the Longridge branch with the Whittingham line was named 'Whittingham Junction'. (Lancashire County Council)

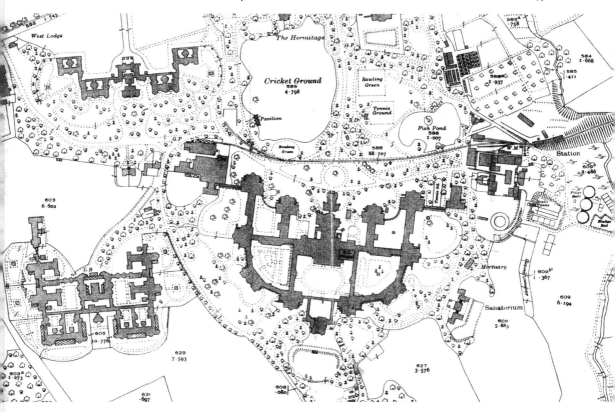

The 25-inch to one-mile Ordnance Survey map of Whittingham from 1938, illustrating the extension of the railway that ran through the hospital's grounds to the boiler house and gas works. The boiler house can be seen attached to the top left of the main complex, St Lukes; the gas works is to the right. To the top left of the boiler house is Cameron House and the West Annexe is bottom left. (Courtesy Lancashire County Council)

to Longridge, a quaint veteran locomotive with a combination of up to three green passenger carriages, bearing an uncanny resemblance to horse boxes, gently simmered in Grimsargh's second railway station. During its sixty-eight-year existence the steam locomotives and stock operating on the totally eccentric Whittingham railway made the old-fashioned steam locomotives on the neighbouring line look like today's equivalent of 'Eurostar'.

The following encounter with *James Fryars* is taken from my recollections of a visit during 1953.

On arrival at Grimsargh Station, we discovered that the entire operational staff on the railway comprised only two separate teams of drivers and firemen. Hence there was no ticket office and anyone could travel. All they provided at Grimsargh was a waiting room, complete with a roaring coal fire and a single electric light bulb. It was rather like the 'Marie Celeste', a ghost station with no staff.

Beneath considerable smoke emissions, an ancient steam engine suddenly appeared around the curve close to Dixon's Farm. As the apparition drew nearer, along rails deeply submerged in a weedy single track, the sight and sound of steam was perceived with a sense of yearning and nostalgia. Upon arrival and after running round its train, I stood in awe at the sight of a truly antiquated steam engine named *James Fryars* and witnessed the early shift of hospital workers slamming the doors of three green carriages, which had been converted from LNWR guard vans by the hospital's joiners.

The kindly engine crew allowed me on the footplate to look at the controls of the clapped out old veteran, affectionately known by them as 'Jimmy Fryar'. To my astonishment, fireman Bennett produced a coal shovel, which was placed above the roaring fire to fry bacon, eggs and field mushrooms for breakfast, washed down with tea from the driver's 'billy can'. I am not too sure about the coal dust, but giant field mushrooms on toast, washed down with tea from the driver's 'billy can', tasted delicious but then even at that age I took the view that if germs can survive such an ordeal they almost deserve to poison you!

A lunch menu of tripe and trotters awaited the crew on the driver's seat. I was informed it was to be doused down with vinegar and pepper; understandably so because, for the uninitiated, the tripe would have once lined a cow's belly, while the trotters originated from the edible (or inedible) parts of a pig's foot! Thanks but no thanks! I pondered that mischievous propensity that once got the better of me and led to the innocuous alteration of the chalked words tripe and trotters displayed on a local shop window. By deleting both letter 't's, it left the poor shopkeeper proudly advertising 'ripe-rotters'. Needless to say, we little urchins ran for it but no damage was done and at least one scoundrel survived the ordeal relatively unscathed.

However, back on the Whittingham train anything could happen! The patented coaches bore an uncanny resemblance to cattle trucks. They even had the luxury of wooden seats around the sides of the carriage and gas central heating provided by a Calor Gas bottle, which was locked away inside the coaches. I am not very sure about the loose coupled conveyances (for want of a better word) having other minor features such as brakes! Nor did the driver need to worry about signals or single line tokens, because on this single track line – without any passing loops apart from the siding at Grimsargh – they simply did not exist and who had ever heard of gradient or mile-post signs? Happily the joint skills of driver and fireman were synchronised as a team in maintaining momentum over the gradients and with a watchful eye from the footplate. There was not a single bridge spanning the Whittingham line, only occupation/footpath crossings and culverts over Savick and Blundell Brooks. The largest structures along the line were two arched stone bridges; the first crossing over Brabiner Lane, the second an occupation overbridge nearby (the latter still *in situ* in 2012).

Suddenly and unannounced there was a jolt and a lurch followed by a blow on the engine's whistle, as the train eased off from the platform to commence the journey to Whittingham. The tiniest of windows allowed us to savour the pleasant countryside during the six-minute journey to Whittingham, which was a fairly comfortable ride as I recall. From Grimsargh Station, the line curved in a north-westerly direction away from the Longridge line, past an exchange siding used to stable British Railway's coal trucks, before reducing to a single track approaching Dixon's Farm. Here, at the first footpath crossing over the line, a family group gave us a friendly wave from lush green fields and the driver gave a reciprocal toot on the engine's whistle.

Meanwhile I was totally mesmerized by the whole experience of the Whittingham line; including riding past tumbling lapwings with the exhaust beat and shrill whistle of the engine competing with joyful chirruping swallows and the evocative calls of curlews echoing over the meadows, not to mention the galloping heifers. The latter had a clear lead over the engine and seemed to be winning an impromptu race. Advancing along a straight downward gradient, the train gained some speed and may even have reached 20 mph while crossing the valley of Savick Brook – perish the thought. After all surely the last thing anyone needed, whether patients, staff or visitors, was a white-knuckle ride! Fortunately I had been reassured by the crew that there had never been a serious accident on the WHR involving personal injury to passengers, only to cattle.

After crossing Savick Brook the train veered slightly right and entered a cutting about thirty to forty feet deep, gloriously festooned with colourful ox-eye daisies and purple orchids to emerge on a high embankment while crossing over Blundell Brook and Brabiner Lane bridge, the largest bridge on the line. This was where my parents took me in Dad's old Morris 8 to watch the train passing by while we enjoyed an afternoon picnic by a cascading waterfall, a scene that somehow harmonised with the rural branch line, adding the icing on the cake to an idyllic country scene. Sadly a scene that is now long gone.

After crossing over the stone Dell Brow bridge, the familiar water tower landmark at Whittingham hospital and the black smoke rising from the boiler-house chimney came into view. One suddenly felt a feeling of *déjà vu* on behalf of successive generations of patients who euphemistically had held a one-way ticket for the journey to the Victorian asylum that the railway line had served since 1889. As the train trundled on towards Whittingham Station it seemed to acquire an unnerving swaying motion whilst negotiating a left-hand curve on a high embankment and where fortunately a check-rail was in place.

Approaching the station, on a rising gradient of 1 in 120, the line passed an abandoned loop line, used to store a collection of antiquated passenger carriages, which I vaguely remember as simply being there. The driver eased off the throttle and the train quietly clanked into the station without further incident. This worthy station building commanded a good view of the hospital's sewage farm – not a real show-stopper as tourist attractions go! Alighting from the train onto the narrow platform we walked past the engine-shed and around an ornamental lake in the hospital grounds. Then, after being attacked by a busking mute swan and watching a cricket match, it was time to walk back to the railway station and experience the return journey, but on this occasion with 'Jimmy Fryar' propelling the train from the rear all the way back to Grimsargh. Maybe the driver had X-ray vision but then in those days who had heard of something called health and safety – it could only have happened on the Whittingham line, I think.

The buffer stops at Grimsargh Station with a few passengers awaiting the next train. The notice on the station building read 'any person found trespassing on the line will be prosecuted'. (N. Evans collection)

Viewed from any angle, the Stroudley D1 0-4-2 *James Fryars* made an alluring sight. On 28 June 1952, the engine is about to depart from Grimsargh Station with its train. (Courtesy of Gordon Biddle)

Grimsargh station showing the D1 Stroudley 0-4-2 with its train of converted brake vans about to depart on 21 April 1951. I rode behind this engine to Whittingham and back. (HCC/RMC)

Shortly after leaving Grimsargh Station, *James Fryars* passes the connecting link with the Longridge branch and heads for Whittingham on 12 April 1952. (Courtesy of Alan Summerfield)

A rural scene at Dixon's Farm: a driver's eye view of the permanent way, looking towards Whittingham on 4 May 1957. (Courtesy of Dorron Harper)

The driver on the footplate of Barclay No. 2 passing through pleasant countryside near Dixon's farm, Grimsargh. (George Whiteman collection)

Steam in the landscape: *Gradwell* is shown Grimsargh-bound with a single van atop the embankment spanning Blundell Brook on 4 May 1957. (Courtesy of Dorron Harper)

Brabiner Lane bridge, complete with warning board on the fence. The bridge was a particularly good example of skew bridge construction. Whittingham Hospital is to the right. (Courtesy of Dorron Harper)

The weed-strewn single track and the bridge spanning Brabiner Lane looking towards Grimsargh. A Ford Popular can just be seen through the trees to the left, proceeding along the lane. (Courtesy of Dorron Harper)

Barclay No. 2 approaches Whittingham Station on a high embankment with a passenger train. (Courtesy of Alan Summerfield)

The view from the train approaching the hospital; the boiler house chimney can be seen and the disused Whittingham siding on the left. A record photograph taken through glass on 12 January 1957. (Courtesy of Dorron Harper)

The ornamental lake in the hospital grounds complete with a motley collection of mallards. (Author's collection)

Grandad Bowman watching a cricket match at Whittingham before boarding the train back to Grimsargh. (Author's collection)

On arrival at Whittingham, the D1 Stroudley *James Fryars* gently simmered in the station yard. (HCC/RMC)

The Whittingham train is shown alongside the platform at Whittingham, ready for departure to Grimsargh. (HCC/RMC)

Above and below: Beyond Whittingham station, the line crossed landscaped lawns and gardens. The top image looks towards the boiler house chimney (centre right) and the bottom image towards Whittingham Station. (HCC/RMC)

Twenty-three years later at the start of the 'swinging 1960s' I was employed at Whittingham Hospital when curiosity beckoned me to follow an old sign 'to the station'. Whittingham Station was by now just a shadow of its former self with the rails long gone and only the track-bed remaining. Thereafter on many glorious spring mornings, I walked the two miles along the track-bed to work at the hospital, and reacquainted myself with the tumbling lapwings and 'larks ascending' happy in the knowledge that just over two decades previously I had travelled on the quaint and unconventional hospital train from Grimsargh to Whittingham and lived to tell the tale. In conclusion, the WHR was indubitably something of a music hall conundrum let alone a music hall joke!

Whittingham Hospital bridge and station entrance today. (Mark Bartlett)

CHAPTER FIVE

Veteran and Vintage Steam Locomotives and Rolling Stock

Surprisingly, throughout its sixty-eight-year existence, the WHR aspired to only four hard-working steam locomotives and details are given below. Early diesels were never acquired for the fleet.

At Whittingham it was typically a case of 'make do and mend', with limited resources and two second-hand steam engines and carriage stock being obtained and adapted for a change of use.

Builder	Class	Year Acquired	Acquired From	Year Disposed
A. Barclay	0-4-0	1888	A. Barclay	1946
A. Barclay	0-4-2	1904	A. Barclay	1952
W. Stroudley	D1 0-4-2T	1947	Southern Rly	1955
Sentinel	0-4-0 4WVBT	1953	Bolton Gasworks	1957

A brand new 0-4-0 saddle-tank engine was the first locomotive to be purchased from Andrew Barclay & Sons, Kilmarnock, in 1888, for the sum of £790. At the same time, two goods vans were ordered to make up its train. Before the advent of motorised travel and because of the hospital's isolation in the Lancashire countryside, the desire to carry staff and patients to the asylum was considered necessary. Despite the committee's remit to convey only freight traffic a four-wheel carriage was purchased in 1889 for £277 10s from the Lancaster Carriage and Wagon Company. Not surprisingly, a single carriage proved to be inadequate for the number of passengers being transported. Therefore, in 1895 two former four-wheeled composite second- and third- class North London Railway carriages were purchased for £180 from the London & North Western Railway. The carriages were easily distinguished by a set of steps at either end, which gave access to the roof. These steps were used for maintenance and by the lamplighter to illuminate the carriage compartments.

The original 0-4-0 Barclay No. 1 of 1888 pauses between trips at Grimsargh Station. (Courtesy of George Whiteman)

Barclay No. 2 crossing over Brabiner Lane bridge on the approach to Whittingham. (George Whiteman collection)

Another view of Barclay No. 1 approaching Whittingham with a mixture of veteran carriages. The third carriage is an L&YR third-class compartment brake complete with 'birdcage' on the roof. (George Whiteman collection)

Barclay 0-4-2 No. 2 leaves Grimsargh Station with original L&YR carriage stock in red and white livery around the time of the Great War. (Courtesy of Mrs Frances Wright)

A close-up view of Barclay No. 2 at Whittingham. (Hospital Archives)

Barclay No. 2 at Grimsargh Station – the engine crew 'take 5'. (Courtesy of Alan Summerfield)

Above and below: On a visit to the WHR by Mr H. Casserley and his son Richard on 21 April 1951, the D1 Stroudley dragged the Barclay 0-4-2 out of the engine shed to be photographed. (HCC/RMC)

Barclay No. 2 passes the weighbridge at Whittingham. (HCC/RMC)

The WHR's ex-Midland railway goods van in the siding at Whittingham on 21 April 1951. It was later cut converted to an open truck for utilitarian use on the WHR. (HCC/RMC)

During the first decades of the twentieth century the passenger accommodation was provided in ex-Lancashire & Yorkshire and North London carriages (the latter with steps at either end). These carriages bore the letters CAW up to 1923 and CMHW thereafter. (Courtesy of Alan Summerfield)

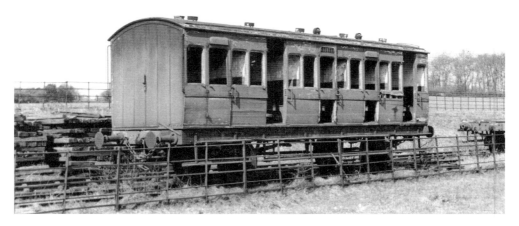

The ex-Lancashire & Yorshire coach stands forlorn at Whittingham on 21 April 1951. Note the stack of old railway sleepers to the left. (HCC/RMC)

Passenger accommodation was provided in classic veteran carriages, here being admired by visiting enthusiasts. They were originally painted red and white but were latterly plain brown. (Courtesy of Alan Summerfield)

A siding at Whittingham harboured the last original disused carriages with more evidence of work on the permanent way; tragically they were destined for scrap. The view of the WHR is looking towards Grimsargh. (HCC/RMC)

The original carriages were superseded by three green converted ex-LNWR guard vans in 1946, as shown here in the yard at Whittingham on 12 January 1957. (Courtesy of Dorron Harper)

Barclay No. 2 takes time off in the siding at Grimsargh station, *c.* 1951. (Courtesy of Alan Summerfield)

Thereafter, a total of three four-wheeled second-hand carriages were purchased from the Lancashire & Yorkshire Railway, two in 1906 and one in 1910. Although the Whittingham line was without a class, the LYR carriages afforded a modicum of luxury, with roof lamps and cushioned seats. The compartments were still marked first, second and third, but this was merely a legacy of the previous owners, for no money was ever exchanged for tickets on the hospital railway. The carriages originally bore the letters CAW up to 1923 and CMHW thereafter. When the PLR passenger service ceased in 1930, the original red and white-liveried carriages were reduced to three, perhaps an indication that there was less of a demand for the Whittingham service.

The antiquated stock of three carriages lasted until 1946, when they were ignominiously shunted into a running loop near Whittingham Station and left to rot. Thereafter, hospital staff and patients, in a rather slapdash fashion in the hospital's workshops, converted three ex-LNWR 20-ton goods brake vans. The modified stock came complete with replacement doors and side seats round the carriage interior. One of the vans retained a handbrake. For passenger comfort, five small windows were fitted and Calor Gas was installed for cold winter journeys, the containers being neatly padlocked inside the coaches.

The hospital's innovative workshop men also converted an ex-Midland railway goods van to an open low-sided wagon, at first intended to carry the bicycles of staff that had cycled to Grimsargh from outlying villages. By the 1950s, however, the passenger carriages were sufficiently commodious to accommodate the cycles and the van was utilised for ballast and general purpose.

During 1904 a second, more powerful Barclay 0-4-2 side tank was purchased from Andrew Barclay & Sons, Kilmarnock to join its sister engine on the WHR. Between the two World Wars, the two Barclay engines were the sole motive power on the line. Regular drivers and firemen manned them. During the 1940/50s two engine crews worked from about 5 a.m. to 1 p.m. and 1 p.m. to 9 p.m. respectively and turns were exchanged on alternate weeks with Driver Whalley and Fireman Dunn and Driver Wright and Fireman Bennett.

Technical Details of the Two Barclay Locomotives

Barclay No. 1 (0-4-0 saddle-tank)	Barclay No. 2 (0-4-2 side-tank)
Works number: 304	Works number: 1026
Date purchased: 1888	Date purchased: 1904
Cylinders 13" x 20"	Cylinders 13" x 20"
Coupled wheels 3' 7" diameter	4' 1" diameter, trailing 3' 0" diameter.
Boiler: working pressure 120lbs/sq. in.	Boiler: working pressure 160 lbs/sq. in.
Heating surface: boiler 440 sq. feet	Heating surface: boiler 460 sq. feet
Heating surface: firebox 48 sq. feet	Heating surface: firebox 52 sq. feet
Tank capacities 640 gallons of water	Tank capacities 640 gallons of water

Weight loco. Empty: 19 ton 5 cwt	Weight loco. Empty: 21 ton 5cwt
Weight loco. Loaded: 23 ton 5 cwt	Weight loco. Loaded: 25 ton

With the demise of Barclay No. 1 in 1946, a replacement engine was urgently sought. Approaches to the railway companies were made for a suitable machine and the Southern Railway offered an old Stroudley 0-4-2 (T) class D1, originally No. 357. The locomotive, withdrawn in 1944, was even older than the line, having been manufactured in 1886 and, not surprisingly, it was the sole survivor of its class. William Stroudley was Chief Mechanical Engineer of the LBSCR and designer of this particular locomotive, which bore the name *Riddlesdown*, after the location it originally served. Up to the 1920s, such engines worked on London suburban lines but, as electrification developed, most of the survivors were fitted for push-and-pull working in country areas.

In February 1947, the D1 was purchased for Whittingham at a cost of £750, for immediate operational use as CMHW No 1. This acquisition coincided with pre-nationalisation, when many veterans of the 'iron road' were destined for scrap. When the engine arrived at Whittingham, it still bore the Southern nameplate of *Riddlesdown*, and the words 'Southern Railway'. In October 1947, during a ceremony at Whittingham Hospital Station, the locomotive was named *James Fryars*, in honour of a chairman of the hospital visiting committee. Amid clouds of steam from his namesake, Alderman Fryar gave a brief history of the railway to the assembled

The manufacturer's work-plate of the second Barclay of 1904. (Courtesy of George Whiteman)

committee. Mr W. A. Higgs (hospital management) then announced the benefits of the latest engine and alluded to the free railway.

> In addition to ten double journeys each day, hauling passenger trains the locomotive will be used for bringing vital goods traffic to the hospital. An average of 12,000 tons of coal and slack is brought along the railway from Grimsargh each year, as well as hundreds of tons of other goods. The passenger service is entirely free, and carries more than 200 of the hospital staff to and from Grimsargh daily. The service is also used by visitors to patients at the hospital.

Alderman Fryar mentioned the replacement converted passenger carriages. 'Three brake vans have been acquired from the LMS and are now fitted out as passenger carriages.'

With Driver Whalley and Fireman Young on the footplate, he then led the committee for a guided tour of the line behind his namesake locomotive to Grimsargh.[18] Afterwards, Fireman Young said, 'Jimmy Fryar's all right on the straight, but she grinds a bit on the bends.' The locomotive was said to be so powerful that the regulator needed minimal opening throughout the journey. The journey time from Grimsargh to Whittingham Station depended on the capability of the particular locomotive. The D1 took on average about six minutes to complete the journey, though it was well capable of doing the journey in three to four minutes.

The Stroudley was to survive for less than ten years, for, by 1955, the engine was suffering from serious internal disorders (blocked tubes) and there was no one to perform major surgery at the hospital in respect of a condemned boiler! Consequently, about two years before the Whittingham line closed, the engine took a one-way ticket to a siding and stood forlornly outside the shed in terminal decline. Following closure of the line in 1957, the remains of this iconic locomotive were sold for scrap for a mere £350 to a merchant at Wigan.

Unfortunately, the Stroudley tank's demise preceded the railway preservation era, yet among many steam-locomotive enthusiasts, the memory of the D1 is still revered. It was as a direct result of the loss of such locomotives and branch lines in the 1960s that the heritage railway movement was born and, with it, the acquisition of redundant locomotives and former branch lines. With hindsight, if only we had known then what we know now!

Following the demise of Barclay No. 2 in 1952, a replacement engine was urgently sought. It transpired that in 1953 a driver was instructed to 'go to Bolton Gas-works to pick up an engine'. The fourth and final acquisition had been built at the Sentinel wagon works, Shrewbury in 1947, works number 9377, as a 0-4-0 Sentinel 100 hp steam engine. In fact, *Gradwell* was still resplendent with the emblem of Bolton Corporation on the dummy boiler casing. The vertical water-tube boiler was in the cab. The diminutive engine was capable of hauling the three passenger carriages without effort, or up to about thirty twelve-ton wagons, weighing around 360 tons. With a modest running speed of only 13 mph, *Gradwell* operated the service almost single-handed during the final year of the railway's existence and just about maintained the status quo.

Class D1 0-4-2 side tank, originally No. 357 (later 2357), formerly worked on the London, Brighton & South Coast Railway. It is seen here at New Cross Gate on 4 March 1939. (HCC/RMC)

Another view of the Stroudley Class D1 0-4-2 side tank in Southern livery. (HCC/RMC)

Class D1 0-4-2, seen here at Pulborough in Southern region livery as No. 357 on 30 August 1930, with the 11.00 train to Midhurst. (HCC/RMC).

The D1 at Guildford on 3 September 1932, as Southern No. 2357. The engine was transferred to Whittingham in 1947. (HCC/RMC)

The antiquated engine 'up from the smoke': on 12 April 1952, the unique ex-London, Brighton & South Coast Railway 0-4-2 Stroudley D1, now re-named *James Fryars*, is ready to leave Grimsargh Station with the 5.20 p.m. train to Whittingham on 12 April 1952. (Courtesy of Alan Summerfield)

James Fryars with a single carriage propelling its train along the embankment to Grimsargh. (George Whiteman collection)

Whittingham engine shed with the boiler of the Stroudley standing forlornly, ultimately destined for scrap. The rest of the engine was inside the shed. (N. Evans collection)

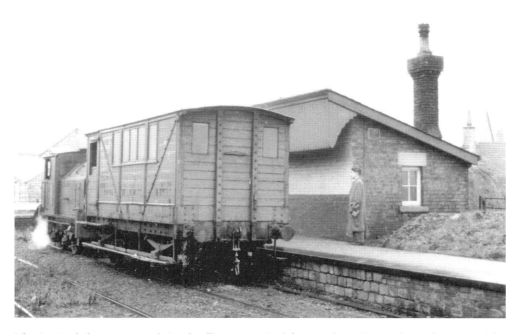

The Sentinel shunter, named *Gradwell*, was acquired from Bolton Gas-works in the 1950s. The engine is shown alongside a deserted Grimsargh Station with a single carriage, epitomising the rural branch line. (Tom Heginbotham collection)

Journey's end as the Sentinel crosses over the embankment on the approach to Whittingham station with its single carriage. (Courtesy of Alan Summerfield)

Sentinel locomotive *Gradwell* lets off steam in the picturesque grounds of Whittingham Hospital on 1 June 1957. (Courtesy N. Evans collection)

Following complete closure of the WHR in June 1957, the Sentinel gained pastures new in north-east England when sold to Messrs G. Stephenson, builders and contractors of Bishop Auckland, who in turn resold it in 1958 to the Tyne Tees Shipping Company of Stockton-on-Tees, where it later worked at Vulcan Street Wharf in Middlesbrough. The engine had been given a new lease of life, but was finally scrapped in 1968, eleven years after departure from the Whittingham line. A preserved Sentinel, very similar to *Gradwell*, may be seen at the Ribble Steam Railway, Preston.

There are spurious claims that a Whittingham engine was buried on site, although in my view tangible evidence is almost certainly lacking; until, that is, someone discovers the Holy Grail! What is not in dispute is that had the Whittingham line survived, it would have become a 'Mecca' for railway enthusiasts from far and wide.

A close-up of *Gradwell* and passenger stock at Whittingham. The locomotive was named after Alderman James Gradwell (Bolton Gasworks Committee Chairman). (N. Evans collection)

CHAPTER SIX

Operational Matters

The WHR was operated under the control of the Chief Mechanical Engineer at Whittingham, but on occasions, wayward trains required a degree of supervision. The Reverent W. Audrey would probably have gained further inspiration for his writings of *Thomas the Tank Engine* books had he visited Whittingham, with his creative character the 'Fat Controller', and taken on board the operational functions in running a railway, beginning with an examination of the stations.

The Stations

In the overall scheme of events, the passenger service emerges as something of an afterthought and one for which only basic facilities were provided. Grimsargh's WHR station exemplified a period country branch bay terminus and was complete with a run-round loop, a connection with the PLR and two sidings to facilitate freight interchange. The connection to the Longridge branch was worked from a ground-frame released by an Annett's key placed in the frame, to enable shunting or traffic movement. Grimsargh Station building was some forty feet in length and twelve feet wide, with a ten-foot waiting room at the Longridge end. In 1910, during the peak of passenger services, the platform was given a wooden extension, which was transformed into a substantial structure 218 feet long in 1918. Apart from these modifications, Grimsargh Station then remained virtually in its original form until the line closed in 1957.

A new Whittingham Station was built around 1907 for approximately £500, the undertaking being funded by the Lancashire Asylums Board. The contrast between the styles of station-building was obvious. Whittingham Station was unexpected, because of its peculiar construction of brick with iron pillars supporting an overall glass roof about 150 feet long, enabling the station to be used as a carriage shed. Steps led up onto a narrow single platform and waiting room. The curvature alongside the platform was said to be so sharp that it restricted the use of bogie carriages; therefore, throughout its existence, only four-wheeled carriages were used on the line. Both Grimsargh and Whittingham Stations were precursors to the unstaffed halts of today and remained permanently unmanned throughout their existence.

Grimsargh Station in June 1948, with the LNWR station behind the semaphore signal. Hospital workers board the train for Whittingham hauled by Barclay engine No. 2. (Tom Heginbotham collection)

Grimsargh WHR Station with two prospective passengers. The run-round loop features with mixed freight stock in the siding beyond. (HCC/RMC)

The elaborate Whittingham station, with two waiting passengers on 1 May 1954, photographed by D. Thompson. (Gordon Biddle collection)

The Nerve Centre of Operations

The nerve centre of operations was the station yard, which we always knew as the engineer's yard. On entering the yard, the single track crossed over a weighbridge platform, next to a small brick hut where wagons were separately weighed before being authorised to proceed to the respective power plants. The first set of points were operated by the engine crew and led right to the engine-shed, which first opened in 1906. The single-road engine-shed could accommodate two steam engines and was provided with appropriate machinery for the hospital's engineers. It did, however, lack such basic facilities as a water tower and it appears that, instead, a hose-pipe was used. At first, coaling the engine was done the hard way, with plenty of muscle power and good old Lancashire elbow grease. Latterly, the crew enjoyed the luxury of a conveyor-belt that shifted the coal direct from a commodious supply to the steam engine's bunker.

The WHR owed its origins to the carrying of fossil fuels to the hospital's gas-works and boiler-house. The gas-works and boiler-house were situated at the western and eastern extremities of the hospital's grounds respectively and both were linked by rail. Ordnance Survey Maps clarify the route leading from the station yard via a complex of buildings to the gas-works. Owing to restricted space between buildings, two short turntables were installed for wagons to be turned through an angle of ninety degrees, before being propelled to the gas-works. The centre road led to the engine-shed siding and latterly through the picturesque hospital grounds. It was only in 1922 that the line was extended 520 yards across the lawns to a new boiler-house. The project

Whittingham engine shed with a coal truck in the shed siding. (Hospital Archives)

A view of Whittingham goods yard, with the weighbridge in the foreground and the engine shed to the right. The central road continued to run through the hospital grounds to the boiler-house. The original engine shed was the building at the top left. (Hospital Archives)

'Driver, watch that smoke.' A delightful study of *James Fryars* bracing himself for the 2-mile, white-knuckle ride to Whittingham. (HCC/RMC)

James Fryars proceeds along the extension through the hospital grounds, past the ornamental lake. (Tom Heginbotham collection)

A rare image of *Gradwell* with a coal train heading from Grimsargh to Whittingham. (Courtesy N. Evans collection)

A coal train in the hospital grounds on the final approach to the boiler house. (Tom Heginbotham collection)

cost £3,200 and included a short siding that was used for shunting coal wagons to a reserve supply of coal situated near the cricket field. Apart from special trains run for enthusiasts, passenger trains from Grimsargh never went beyond Whittingham Station, as the extension was for goods trains only. The additional track to the boiler-house provided a total length of 3,386 yards (3,096 metres) from Grimsargh Station.

A Message to the Fat Controller at Whittingham – 'Watch that Smoke'

Throughout the Edwardian era, road transport had yet to make its impact as a serious competitor for the railway. But who would have thought of congestion problems at Grimsargh, said to be a 'great public nuisance' and caused by the asylum railway, as early as 1904?

> At the time it was resolved that the clerk of Grimsargh with Brockholes Parish Council should write to the railway company pointing out the delay to traffic, through closing the gates on the level crossing adjoining Grimsargh Station, and the measure of time taken by shunting operations on the asylum railway. Some attention be given to stop what at present is a great public nuisance.

The Fat Controller (Chief Mechanical Engineer) was again called upon in June 1926, when Grimsargh Parish Council presided over the serious incidence of the smoke and coal dust from the Whittingham Asylum train. The Barclay engine seemed to be beyond control, as it languished in the bay platform at Grimsargh after being stoked up, waiting its next turn of duty. It was said to be like a smoking volcano about to erupt.

> It was brought to the attention of the chairman that something had to be done about those black blemishes on the white sheets floating on washing lines. It was resolved: that the clerk should write to those in charge to fire the train up outside the station.

The Working Timetable

The passenger service peaked during the first decades of the twentieth century. During its 1918 heyday, the Whittingham train carried about 3,000 passengers per week and more than 12,000 tons of freight per annum. Throughout its existence, trains were often mixed, with goods and passenger vehicles running together. There were twelve daily passenger trains operating in each direction, the first leaving Whittingham at 6.10 a.m. and the final departure from Grimsargh at 9.35 p.m. Extra trains ran on Saturdays for the visitors, but in all probability there was never a Sunday or Bank Holiday service. At the time of peak operations, it was not uncommon for the train to carry 200 passengers on Saturday afternoons.

With the provision of a direct Ribble bus service from Preston to Whittingham in 1951, passenger numbers began to decline, reflected in the 1951 WHR timetable (below) although extra trains were still provided on Saturday afternoons for hospital visitors.

Grimsargh to Whittingham (weekdays)	Whittingham to Grimsargh (weekdays)
6.35 a.m., 7.30 a.m., 8.40 a.m., 12.30 p.m., 1.30 p.m. (SO), 2.30 p.m. (SO), 5.20 p.m., 6.30 p.m., 7.20 p.m.	6.10 a.m., 7.10 a.m., 8 a.m., 11.50 a.m. (SO), 1.7 p.m. (SO), 1.30 p.m. (SX), 2 p.m. (SO), 4.35 p.m. (SO), 5 p.m. (SX), 5.40 p.m., 7.10 p.m.

During the quiet morning period, the timetable made provision for the daily freight train, which left Whittingham at approximately 10.00 a.m. with empty goods wagons and usually returned from Grimsargh at 11.30 a.m. with loaded coal wagons.

Ghastly Accidents along the Permanent Way

Throughout the hospital grounds, special precautions had to be taken to protect the public and patients from oncoming trains. The Fat Controller insisted that engine crews had to remain especially vigilant and to keep ceaseless watch for vehicles and pedestrians crossing the line, which necessitated the trains moving very slowly and the fireman preceding the locomotive as a walking pilot. During September 1894, a fatal accident occurred when a train struck a male patient near Whittingham Station and four years later, a hospital patient committed suicide on the line. The gruesome circumstances were duly reported in the local press:

> Shortly before seven o'clock on Thursday night, as the Whittingham Asylum train was proceeding from Grimsargh Station to the asylum, a man supposed to be an escaped lunatic suddenly rushed before the engine, and laid his head on the line. Before the driver could apply his brakes the engine had passed over the neck, shockingly mutilating the body. The body was picked up and taken to the asylum.

The job of maintaining the not-so-permanent way was also assigned to the Controller by way of delegation. During the Second World War, the track infrastructure degenerated and, in 1947, 1,048 yards of track were re-laid and 1,798 yards of track re-sleepered, at a cost of £7,050. Major work on the permanent way combining the partial re-laying of sleepers and rail was also undertaken in 1922, 1930 and for the last time in 1952. The track was generally maintained in good condition and had check-rails on the severe curves. Some of the sidings were not replaced and the seven-hundred-foot-long loop near Whittingham Station, installed around 1912, appears to have been the oldest part of the line.

Barclay No. 2 negotiates Whittingham Junction and begins the two-mile journey along a floral, overgrown single track. (Courtesy of George Whiteman)

The 'push me, pull you' train – *James Fryars* is seen propelling its train from Whittingham to Grimsargh on 25 June 1952. (Courtesy of Gordon Biddle)

A Music Hall Quandary for the Fat Controller Concerning the Push Me Pull You Train

Up to 1951, a primitive system of push-and-pull working operated on the WHR. Passenger trains were always hauled from Grimsargh to Whittingham with the engine at the front of the train. As there was no station loop or turntable at Whittingham yard, it was the practice for the engine to simply push the train back to Grimsargh from the rear of the train, but without the driver having adequate vision from the leading carriage. Elsewhere, of course, it was the practice on conventional branch line trains to adopt a method of push-and-pull working, with a duplicate set of controls being fitted to the leading coach.

Subsequently, this led to the Whittingham train having an unsavoury reputation with local farmers and livestock, following an accident at a cattle crossing on 2 September 1950. The serenity of the idyllic countryside was shattered when a train hit three exuberant heifers that had wandered onto the track from the crossing serving Brabiner House Farm. One beast was killed outright and the other two had to be destroyed and despatched to the knackers' yard. In 1951, the farmer claimed damages and a County Court judge made certain recommendations.

It was the lack of proper resources at Whittingham for turning the engine that led to this accident. Hence it was therefore decreed that basic turn-round facilities at Whittingham should ideally be provided to place the engine at the front of the train. On this most basic of railway lines, however, it seemed to be a question of making use of limited resources and at first the run-round manoeuvre was achieved by means of utilising a method at the cutting edge of technology – a tow-rope! In later years the marvels of modern technology were again invoked with the judicious use of a hoover-like noisy contraption known as a BSA 'wagon mover'.

This ingenious equipment was petrol-driven and had handlebars and rubber wheels that ran on one rail with the crew walking alongside and controlling its movement. (Not surprisingly it is now an exhibit at the National Railway Museum.) Running round the train was then achieved by uncoupling the engine at Whittingham. While the engine entered the shed road for service, the fireman produced the motorised pusher and drove it along the rails until it coupled with the carriage. The fireman then engaged the clutch of the contraption and pushed the three carriages into the carriage road to enable the engine to regain its rightful place at the head of the train. Following the County Court judgement in 1951 the train was run in both directions with the engine at the front. The driver could now enjoy his Sunday joint of roast beef with a clear conscience, without the worry of having sent curious bovines to the knacker's yard!

Wartime Service

The WHR and the Longridge branch both feature in the history of two World Wars. During the Great War wounded soldiers were treated at Whittingham Hospital. St Margaret's was evacuated as an asylum and turned over to the military for their use

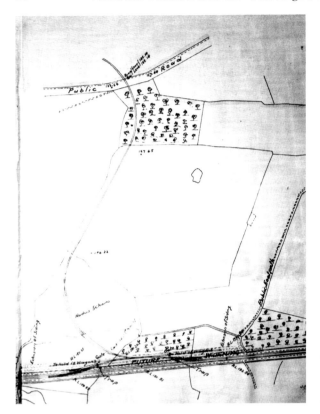

Original plan of the junction of the Calderstones Hospital Railway with the Blackburn to Clitheroe line. (Courtesy Blackburn Museum)

in the care of sick and injured soldiers. There are four graves in the hospital cemetery which are under the care of the War Graves Commission relating to casualties of the First World War.

With the outbreak of the Second World War the rural villages of Grimsargh and Goosnargh played a part in the evacuation of hundreds of thousands of urban children to the countryside of Britain. A special main line train hauling many carriages steamed into the closed LMS Grimsargh Station only two weeks after the outbreak of war. The evacuees from the Manchester area had labels on their collars with their names on so that brothers and sisters would not be separated. The children were processed at the Grimsargh Assembly Hall and provided with local accommodation. Because of overcrowding at Grimsargh St Michael's School, a letter had been sent to the Hospital Management, requesting that the Whittingham trains be used to link with future diagrams arriving at Grimsargh, in order to convey the overspill of evacuees to the village school at Goosnargh. However, the unfortunate children were deemed one group that were to be excluded from the Whittingham trains, on the grounds that 'it is inadvisable that the hospital railway be used as a means of conveyance for these children'.

Perhaps surprisingly the Whittingham Hospital Railway was one of two such hospital railways in Lancashire, the other serving Whalley Asylum, which was the last of six such hospitals to be built in Lancashire. Following the commencement of the

Great War in August 1914, Whalley Asylum became a military hospital for wounded troops. The transformed hospital duly opened in April 1915, with capacity for 2,000 patients, and was named Queen Mary's Military Hospital. A station was built for the exclusive use of the war wounded and trains arrived almost immediately, hauled by the hospital's own fireless steam locomotive, which operated along a short branch off the Blackburn to Hellifield main line. The hospital station comprised of two wooden shelters and platforms with gently sloping ramps either side of the single-track railway.

The half-mile-long hospital branch carried wounded troops from the battlefields of the Great War, but no passengers thereafter. After the First World War the hospital remained under military control until 1921, reverting to its original intended use as a mental hospital, which subsequently became known as Calderstone's Hospital in 1929. By now it had capacity for 3,000 beds and employed about 1,000 staff. The private railway continued in use for the carriage of coal and other goods until modernisation of the boiler house in 1953 and preceding the closure of the hospital. Today a bridge over a cutting on Mitton Road, Whalley remains as a legacy to a railway that was once witness to so much heartbreak and turmoil.

CHAPTER SEVEN

Gone But Not Forgotten

This chapter describes several excursions on the branch and the events leading up to the permanent closure of the WHR on 29 June 1957.

Special Excursion on 1 May 1954

Both the Longridge and Whittingham branches were popular with enthusiasts and a number of specials ran along both tracks during the decade before closure. Members of the Stephenson and Manchester locomotive societies visited the Longridge and Whittingham lines on 1 May 1954. The 1954 visit was part of the North Lancashire Rail Tour. For an inclusive price of ninety shillings there was an opportunity to travel behind a Fowler class 4MT 2-6-2 tank locomotive, No. 42316, along several closed branch lines including Garstang–Pilling, Lancaster–Glasson Dock, Arnside–Hincaster Junction and the Preston to Longridge branch. Optional arrangements were made for those passengers desirous of travelling on the WHR behind the D1 0-6-2 Stroudley from Grimsargh to Whittingham and return.

A special day excursion ticket was issued for the 'North Lancashire Rail Tour', which included the Longridge and Whittingham branch lines. An extract from the joining instructions read as follows:

> The visit to the Whittingham railway has been made possible through the kindness of the hospital authorities, and M. T. Smith, group engineer. Special transport to Grimsargh has been arranged. Buses leave the forecourt of Preston Station 11.30 a.m. and 12.30 p.m. ... A small charge of approximately two shillings will be made to cover the cost of transport and expenses on the Whittingham line. The promoting societies wish to take this opportunity of placing on record their sincere appreciation of the hospital authority's action in placing their line at our disposal for two hours. Parties will also be conducted over other engineering installations on the site.

The joint Stephenson Locomotive Society and Manchester Locomotive Society rail tour of 1 May 1954 arrives at Longridge station behind Crewe North depot's Fowler Class 4MT 2-6-4T No 42316. (Courtesy of Gordon Biddle)

The D1 Stroudley D1 0-4-2, named *James Fryars*, at Grimsargh bound for Whittingham with the special excursion of 1 May 1954. (Courtesy of Gordon Biddle)

The D1 on its arrival at Whittingham Station with the enthusiasts' special on 1 May 1954. Today it would have been a collector's piece, destined for the Bluebell Railway or the National Railway Museum. (Courtesy of R. H. Hughes, Manchester Locomotive Society)

James Fryars passes alongside the lake in the grounds of Whittingham Hospital with the special train for enthusiasts on 1 May 1954. (Courtesy of R. H. Hughes, Manchester Locomotive Society)

James Fryars in tranquil surroundings by the side of the lake on 1 May 1954, complete with interested admirers. (Tom Heginbotham collection)

The D1 *James Fryars*, with nameplate above the inscription 'CMHW No. 1', pauses at Whittingham on 1 May 1954. (Courtesy of R. H. Hughes, Manchester Locomotive Society)

James Fryars joins sister engine *Gradwell* on the shed road at Whittingham on 1 May 1954. (Tom Heginbotham collection)

Enthusiast's Special on Saturday 1 June 1957

On 1 June 1957, sixty enthusiasts on a farewell tour sponsored by three locomotive societies visited the Whittingham line. Two return trips were made with *Gradwell* at the head of the train, which consisted of the three usual passenger brake vans and two open wagons adapted for passengers. Stranger than fiction, in these days of health and safety awareness and perhaps the only place in the world where the passenger trains were regularly hauled by an unorthodox geared Sentinel locomotive – yet another first for this unique line.

The Ultimate End of the Line

By 1956, following the withdrawal of the D1 locomotive, a replacement engine to work alongside *Gradwell* was inconceivable. Consequently, it was with some sadness and reluctance on the part of the Whittingham Hospital Management Committee that a decision was made to close the line in January 1957. Although the railway was said to be conveying some 200-hospital employees each day, loading was down to single figures on certain journeys, with only one carriage being used. The railway cost about £5,000 per annum to run and road haulage of coal direct to the hospital's boilers was considered to be more cost-effective. However, owing to the Suez Crisis and consequential petrol rationing, hospital management waited for the international crisis to subside and in the interim gave the line two reprieves, but this only stalled the inevitable closure.

Throughout June, *Gradwell* was draped with bunting, culminating in a commemorative special train for VIPs on 27 June. The proud little engine carried a special board in front of the boiler proclaiming its heritage – 'Whittingham Railway 1887–1957'. The very last passenger train, hauled by *Gradwell*, ran from Grimsargh to Whittingham on 29 June 1957.

There was hardly any ceremony for the last scheduled train to depart from Grimsargh to Whittingham. Nevertheless, a feeling of sadness prevailed for a small group of about twenty nurses and relatives of the train crew and just a few more onlookers, one of whom was 'yours truly'. As Driver Gilbert Wright opened the regulator and sounded a somewhat melancholy whistle on the 7.20 p.m. to Whittingham, the Sentinel steam engine chugged away into history. The event was modestly commemorated by several fog signals that simultaneously exploded on the single track, by now woven into the pleasant undulating landscape of Lancashire, but not for much longer. Thereafter *Gradwell* was temporarily engaged on the demolition of the historic line, which was completed by 1958.

Gradwell with a single van on arrival at Grimsargh Station. Foreground is the former MR van by now cut down to a wagon. Good view of the connecting link with Longridge branch line and just-visible coal empties placed for return by British Railways on 4 May 1957. (Courtesy of Dorron Harper)

The boiler of the Stroudley D1 0-4-2 in the yard at Whittingham on 4 May 1957. (Courtesy of Dorron Harper)

Gradwell at Grimsargh Station with a single van about to commence its journey to Whittingham on 4 May 1957. (Courtesy of Dorron Harper)

Gradwell and driver Gilbert Wright in the yard at Whittingham on 4 May 1957. (Courtesy of Dorron Harper)

The arrival at Grimsargh of an enthusiast's special on Saturday 1 June 1957, consisting of all three passenger vans and two BR wooden open wagons, lined for the occasion with sheets of Hessian for the comfort of passengers. The leading wagon is an ex-private owner, the lettering still being visible. (Courtesy of Dorron Harper)

Gradwell and the special train, with its complement of enthusiastic passengers on Grimsargh Station platform. (Tom Heginbotham collection)

Gradwell about to depart from Grimsargh on 1 June 1957. (N. Evans collection)

Gradwell proceeding along the straight towards Savick Brook *en route* to Whittingham. Photographed from the train on 1 June 1957. (Tom Heginbotham collection)

The shunting of the stock at Grimsargh of the special train. (Courtesy Dorron Harper)

Gradwell and the special train, letting off steam in the picturesque grounds of Whittingham Hospital. (N. Evans collection)

Grimsargh Station, completely empty though not yet closed, on Thursday 13 June 1957. Rumour has it that many late-night station branch line manoeuvres took place within the station precincts and there was even love 'on line'. (Courtesy of Dorron Harper)

Gradwell crosses over Brabiner Lane bridge, Whittingham bound, on Thursday 13 June 1957. (Courtesy of Dorron Harper)

The same train disappearing towards the final curve and climb to Whittingham on Thursday 13 June 1957. (Courtesy of Dorron Harper)

On Saturday 29 June 1957, *Gradwell* is shown in the yard at Whittingham displaying the final day commemorative headboard, ready to commence the very last return journey. (Courtesy of Dorron Harper)

On the last day of the Whittingham line, the little train was suitably adorned with bunting and is shown here near Dixon's Farm. (Courtesy of Dorron Harper)

Gradwell bows out – Final Curtain Call for the WHR with the 7.20 p.m. train from Grimsargh to Whittingham on Saturday 29 June 1957. Driver Gilbert Wright is on the footplate (with admirer) while Fireman Bennett waits on the platform. (Courtesy of Mrs Frances Wright)

Gradwell blew its whistle and there was plenty of smoke of steam as it passed by Dixon's Farm, Grimsargh. Who was the little boy peering out of the carriage window, one wonders? (Courtesy of Dorron Harper)

This atmospheric photograph again portrays *Gradwell* on the last journey to Whittingham on Saturday 29 June 1957, suitably adorned with a headboard encapsulating the line's history. (Photographed by Dr G. P. Reed M.B., Medical Officer of British Railways)

At the end of the day on Saturday 29 June 1957, Gradwell entered the engine shed at Whittingham and is shown here standing behind the cab, bunker and chassis of the LBSCR Stroudley D1 0-4-2. If only we knew then what we know now the latter would have been a prime candidate for preservation. (Courtesy of Dorron Harper)

Whittingham Revisited

While walking across the remains of the historic track-bed near Dixon's Farm, I still recall that June evening with dreamlike images of a hissing and puffing snake-like train writhing away round the double bends, to the accompaniment of a number of exploding detonators. Into the sunset it went for the very last time, recalling a bygone railway age that had existed since Victorian times. Today a few scars left on the landscape and a black corroded iron fence belies the course of the railway. Footpath crossings and stiles still give access to the track-bed, where agricultural land now reaches out across to reclaim the former railway. The bridge over Brabiner Lane lasted until demolition in 1978 and a stone-arched bridge at Dell Brow still survives intact near to Brabiner Lane, where certain earthworks over the middle section remain intact. Both stations have long since disappeared, although the derelict Whittingham Station did survive until the 1980s.

Post-war pharmacological advancement and reform saw improvements for the treatment of mental illness. The Mental Health Act of 1960, and subsequent legislation, triggered the eventual closure of large Victorian institutions. Whittingham Hospital was closed completely on 31 March 1995, and most of the complex has now been demolished. Consequently there is little evidence of the railway within the hospital grounds.

Three months after closure of the line, Brabiner Lane bridge is shown on 21 September 1957 on a damp open day with the track still in place. (Courtesy of Dorron Harper)

Grimsargh level crossing gates showing the steep gradients beyond the signal on the road to Longridge and the joint LNWR/L&YR station adjacent to the crossing (right). At the time, the Grimsargh (WHR) station site (left) was being redeveloped for housing. (Courtesy of Tony Gillett)

Today this fence passing Dixon's Farm at Grimsargh broadly represents the course of the WHR. (David Hindle)

Billy on the old track-bed of the WHR near to Dixon's Farm, Grimsargh. The original iron railings are still in situ. (David Hindle)

Brabiner Lane bridge, seen here before demolition but with the rails long removed and, speaking from personal experience of walking the line to work, by now a well-used footpath. (Courtesy of Dorron Harper)

Dell Brow bridge, on the approach to Whittingham, is today the only substantial structure remaining. (David Hindle)

The Whittingham Hospital Railway track-bed above the extant Dell Brow overbridge in 2010. (David Hindle)

This long-abandoned overbridge covered with vegetation crossed over a minor road leading to the sewage farm (phew) and has since been demolished. (David Hindle)

All that was left of Whittingham Station in 1960, looking towards the hospital grounds. (Courtesy of Tony Gillett)

The remains of Whittingham Station in 1960, looking towards Grimsargh. (Courtesy of Tony Gillett)

Alongside a completely overgrown track-bed are several concrete blocks that once formed the base of Whittingham Station, providing the only remaining evidence of the station by 2005. (David Hindle)

In Whittingham yard the old engine shed is still recognisable, though it has taken on a new lease of life. (David Hindle)

The derelict shell of the handsome St Luke's main hospital building at Whittingham Hospital, awaiting demolition in 2008. During 1960 I was employed in this building – how things have changed! (David Hindle)

The Plough Inn at Grimsargh was originally Grimsargh's first railway station. The Langden Fold housing development (left) has now been built on the site of the WHR station. (David Hindle)

The derelict main hospital buildings at Whittingham in 2012. (Mark Bartlett)

CHAPTER EIGHT

Brief Encounters and Love On-line

The final chapter contains anecdotal and personal recollections, corresponding with a degree of unashamed nostalgia. My memories of the Whittingham line are described in Chapter Four. My fondest memory of the Longridge branch was to ride on the footplate of the last steam locomotive from Courtaulds to Lostock Hall, on Friday 2 August 1968, which also marked the last day of full-scale steam freight operations on British Railways and was actually the penultimate day before the official cessation of steam. Lostock Hall continued as a working depot until the end of steam in 1968, thereby eclipsing Preston shed, which closed as a result of a disastrous fire occurring on 28 June 1960. Long before the days of modern traction and multiple units, I ventured onto the hallowed ground of Preston engine shed. What a filthy, oily, sooty yet fabulous place this really was, with engines such as 49191 and 49196 on home ground, yet just yards away from their principal haunt, on the line to Longridge. A lasting memory of the site was seeing rows of withdrawn Patriot class locomotives and the superb engine 46257 *City of Salford* (with the inscription 'To Crewe for scrap' crudely chalked on the buffers) all lined up ignominiously pending their fate for, regrettably, there was to be no railway Valhalla for any of these particular splendid locomotives after many years at the sharp end.

As the memories come flooding back, retired Wing Commander Alan Wilding shared with me his own recollections of the Whittingham line:

> I remember, as a small boy in the 1930s, that we set off for a trip on the small steam train, which then plied between Grimsargh and Whittingham Mental Hospital, for a walk in the hospital's grounds and to see a pantomime in the hospital ballroom. This was my first ever train ride and the train trip was the real object of the visit. I recall that the service was used for a few passengers and bulk freight to the hospital.

During the untroubled glory days of the Whittingham line and long before the digital, mobile and satellite video days, it was indeed funny old trains that helped to characterise the local branch that was fully integrated into the landscape. This was at a time when the pastoral countryside between Grimsargh and Whittingham was augmented during haymaking time with a workforce armed with swishing scythes

An old-fashioned farmhouse, similar to the one which stood at Moss Nook. 'Although Moss Nook had been a farmhouse, we only kept poultry and a gaggle of white geese.' (Courtesy Alan Wilding)

and plenty of muscle and energy. Mrs Annie Whiteside resided at Moss Nook Farm, Grimsargh, close to the WHR, and reminisced about the halcyon farming days of Grimsargh in the 1920s mirroring simple pleasures and a long-gone way of life in villages such as Grimsargh that was fortuitously linked to the outside world at 'Whittingham Junction':

Open a five-barred gate, walk down a path to the front door which had a trellis porch covered with rambler roses, and into the comfortable living room. We had a big open range on which we burned huge logs in winter, as it was difficult for the coalman to come often, due to the poor access. At one side of the house we had a well; such clear, cold water. There would be twenty or thirty bright green frogs round the well,the front garden was a riot of sweet-smelling flowers and plants. On summer nights we all liked to sit out on our rustic seat and enjoy the perfume of the flowers. At haymaking time the scent of new-mown hay would be wafted on the air from the surrounding fields, adding to our enjoyment. We must have sat for hours listening to the lovely song of the blackbirds. It must have been like a bird sanctuary at that time – we had so many birds' nests in our hedges. Naturally we had a Barn Owl from time to time and his familiar call could be heard all night.

In winter it was a different story. The view from all our windows was like a Christmas card – pure driven snow – only the footprints of birds, rabbits, or a vole,

Right and below: The white plumes of smoke that drifted over the fields accompanied by the shrill whistle and exhaust blasts of hard working locomotives contrasted with the charismatic calls of lapwings, curlews and skylarks and the ghostly outline of a barn owl sitting on a post. A lament, perhaps, for the passing of nature and a way of community life that now seems long gone. To the right can be seen a barn owl domiciled at Moss Nook Farm, and below a lapwing with chicks. (Courtesy of Peter Smith)

The passing of an era is represented by this close-up photograph of Barclay No. 2 complete with a corroded chimney and the letters CMHW No. 2. (George Whiteman collection)

Rural bliss: seven weeks before closure a Grimsargh-bound train with a single van approaching Brabiner Lane on 4 May 1957. Note the plate layer's hut. Altogether a forgotten scenario of quaint little trains in a vanishing landscape. (Courtesy of Dorron Harper)

the church spire, and a few cottages in the distance. What lovely winter evenings we had if our friends ventured out to see us. We had a piano and my mother played quite well, and we would all gather round to sing. My father liked to render 'If you were the only girl in the world' and the popular tunes I remember were 'Tea for two', 'One Alone' and excerpts from 'The Merry Widow'. Lots of harmonizing, whether good or bad, no one worried. There was always a huge log fire and we would have roasted chestnuts, potatoes covered in their jackets, or toast. We had oil lamps, sending a soft glow over my mother's beautifully polished brasses. A copper kettle stood on the hob ready to make a warming drink, and for those who desired something stronger there were our home-made wines.

Although 'Moss Nook' had been a farmhouse we only kept poultry and a gaggle of white geese. My bedroom had a wide window-seat; I loved to sit there and gaze out on miles of fields, hedges and trees, and to be able to touch the roses which climbed so high: to be awakened by the dawn chorus of birds, sheep baaing, contented cows lowing, and our own hens and one supercilious cock crowing to show his ladies who was the boss; these memories I cherish dearly. We were all very sad when we had to leave Moss Nook due to my father's work. Sadly, 'Moss Nook' farm, like the nearby railway, has long disappeared from the landscape.

Mrs Ada Wild recalled that when she was a little girl, the kindly engine crew gave her a footplate lift from Grimsargh to an unscheduled stop at her home, Dixon's farm. This could only have happened on the WHR! The vagaries of the timetable depended on the driver, who knew his passengers so well that if anyone missed the train, he would reverse the engine to the station to pick them up. On the WHR there were no intermediate stations, merely a few unscheduled stops. If the old engine ran out of steam, or perhaps between flexible train times, opportunities arose for train crews to gather field mushrooms or to collect wild flowers growing profusely in the cutting next to the line.

For the occupiers of Dixon's Farm, closure of the line in June 1957 was tinged with sadness and fond memories. Gentlemen patients from Whittingham often 'walked the line' and enjoyed a kind welcome at the farm. One patient came into the house and made himself comfortable with a cup of tea, and asked if he might have a wash before walking back to the hospital. Another regular visitor was an elderly gentleman who had no known family. This lonely figure regularly walked to the 'windmill pit', where he spent many happy hours fishing before rounding off his day with a cup of tea at the farm, and walking back along the track to Whittingham.

Meanwhile a certain *General Buller* habitually saw active service in a triangle of fields belonging to Dixon's farmhouse. The esteemed General harmonised well with the steam locomotives ascending the gradients from Grimsargh to Longridge and Whittingham. In the days before agricultural tractors, the General played his part in threshing the grain while contracted out to many local farms. Sadly, the rich tapestry of Grimsargh's countryside and the scent of new-mown hay are long gone, though *General Buller* (steam traction engine No. 2153) survives in private ownership.

Young Nicolas Swarbrick, just a mere 107 years old but surprisingly eloquent and with a lively mind, said in 2001:

As a boy I got used to watching the trains from Whittingham entering and departing from Grimsargh Station, situated at the end of the garden fence at my home, Blackrock Farm, Grimsargh. Across Long Site Lane was the 'main line' passenger station to Preston and Longridge. The sound of the Corncrake uttering its rasping call from deep within the hay meadows served as an alarm clock to get up and catch the 8 a.m. train to Preston. The train stopped at Ribbleton and Deepdale Stations before arriving at Preston Station, from where I walked it to the Catholic Grammar School.

The local 'railway children', too, had a fondness for the WHR and spent their days travelling up and down the line. When they became teenagers they caught the last train of the day on New Year's Eve to attend the Whittingham Ball, held in the hospital's ornate and commodious ballroom. In the early hours of the morning young Nell Noblet and Ester Rigby and friends walked back to Grimsargh, via the most direct route, which was along the track of the hospital railway. At that time of the night the toot of the old steam engine's whistle was replaced by the hoot of a tawny owl calling in the moonlight from a suitable lookout, its weird and wonderful repertoire providing the young ladies with some comfort.

Research has revealed yet more anecdotal material, this time concerning erotic goings on taking place on-line. It seems that love blossomed for quite a few Grimsargh couples within the precincts of Grimsargh's railway station yet a parallel line could hardly be drawn with the famous film *Brief Encounter*. When Trevor Howard met Celia Johnson at Carnforth Railway Station, 30 miles north, so began a little nefarious activity, outwardly innocent and filmed against a background of those wonderful LMS locomotives thundering through Carnforth Station. The renowned station café typically served mugs of tea, plastic facsimile cheese and limp tomato sandwiches. Here, to the accompaniment of Rachmaninov's second piano concerto, a brief encounter progressed favourably, especially when Trevor took his newly found lady friend to the local cinema. When the station clock called time on their flirtations it was time to walk the subway, before catching trains home to respective spouses and presumably they all lived happily ever after!

By contrast Grimsargh never had a cinema and villagers did not need romantic music or double seats, evidenced by fond memories of Grimsargh's senior citizens, who recalled their courting days. It seems that after departure of the last train of the day to Whittingham, many late night branch line manoeuvres took place under Grimsargh's station canopy and in the three carriages that were apparently left unlocked alongside the platform overnight, providing opportunities for amorous courting couples. Indeed, if David Lean had been on location his film would never have got past the censors. It is perhaps as well that the identities of the leading players will assuredly never reach the public domain, though their own memories have been preserved in perpetuity.

There is little doubt that the WHR symbolised a rural railway of a bygone Lancashire in a forgotten scenario of quaint little trains in a vanishing natural landscape, serving a community that seemed lost in the mists of time, when the railway was their only contact with the outside world. I personally discovered life on the inside in January 1960, when I became a member of the hospital's workforce of

A tawny owl looked and sounded quite surreal in the moonlight beside the solitude of the Whittingham tracks. (Courtesy of Peter Smith)

over nine hundred and met a young nurse, Dorothy Shorrock, whom I was destined to marry, and discover there was life beyond the gates of Whittingham after all. I well remember Whittingham as a self-sufficient community with its own farm, churches, joiners and engineer's workshops, butcher's shop, tailor, laundry, sewing department, fire station, commodious ballroom and a wonderful antiquated transport fleet. The latter included the steam railway to Grimsargh, crimson vintage fire engines, a 1940s Bedford charabanc, and a horse-drawn hearse, which was still in regular use for hospital funerals. On these sombre occasions hospital staff swapped their brown work coats for a black topper and suddenly became reverential. Two days a week we boarded the hospital's classic 1940s Bedford bus to be conveyed the five-mile journey to Alston Hall. The fifteen-minute ride on the old coach seemed to stimulate youthful exuberance and raised a few eyebrows in Grimsargh.

Alston Hall was meant to further enrich our education in the science subjects but, alas, some students sustained an appalling lack of commitment! The college skeleton often went on regular walkabouts to take a comfortable seat in the conservatory. The principal of the college, Mr J. Shemilt, took a professional and affectionate interest in each and every one of us. Inspirational and charismatic, there was no subject that failed to challenge his superior intelligence and wit. After the excellent lunch we followed the sounds of Cliff Richard's 'Living Doll' emanating from the college cellar. Shades of the famous Liverpool Cavern but in 1960 nobody had ever heard of the

Alston Hall, where the author studied science at the start of the Swinging Sixties. (Courtesy Alan Wilding)

Beatles. This was unquestionably the launch of the 'swinging 60s', symbolised with famous pop groups and good looking girls dressed fashionably in miniskirts dancing as if there was no tomorrow on the college dance floor.

After a relatively 'brief encounter' at Whittingham, Dorothy was appointed Ward Sister at the old Preston Royal Infirmary and I joined the ranks of the boys in blue at Blackburn. I look back with feelings of misgivings of lost opportunities, and for not taking too many photographs during the heyday of those golden days of steam. The white plumes of smoke that drifted over the fields accompanied by the shrill whistle and exhaust blasts of hard-working locomotives contrasted with the charismatic calls of lapwings, curlews and skylarks. Today such quintessential elements of avian excellence are in free-fall decline and to a certain extent a similar analogy might be applied to the network of local railways that were once pivotal to the rural landscape of England. Furthermore, I am constantly reminded that an English countryside that was once immortalized in music by Hubert Parry and Edward Elgar is these days being transformed by unrelenting agricultural, housing and industrial developments.

A lament, perhaps, for the passing of nature and a way of community life that now seems long gone.

The Dawn Chorus – A Musical Encore

Mrs Annie Whiteside at Moss Nook alluded to those halcyon days at Grimsargh and the 'dawn chorus'. The study of birdsong is a fantastic journey into animal behaviour and their calls and songs may be heard just about anywhere. However, all species had their own part to play in a glorious musical overture which was best heard at dawn during April and May. One must get up very early to hear the unique concert of nature, the dawn chorus, which usually lasts up to half an hour. In fact, metaphorically speaking a good dawn chorus might be imaginatively likened to an orchestral performance, though lead vocalists do not need a maestro's podium here Throughout the centuries composers have been inspired by birdsong and as music as always been an important part of life, I looked forward to the walk along the line all the way from Ribbleton to Grimsargh then along the track to Whittingham while enjoying the dawn chorus. At this time of day common species of birds sang effortlessly and were far more abundant than they are today.

> Therefore I now commend for your utter delectation and delight a whimsical musical encore from the Whittingham line which will be performed by inspired maestros and avian virtuosos, and all superb artists as anyone with an ear for music will concur. Come the dawn – I can't wait!

Listening to Vaughan William's 'A Lark Ascending' makes one ponder how much longer the skylark will be the *prima donna* of the great outdoors as it was fifty years ago at the time of the WHR. Nationally, skylark numbers have plunged by over a million in the past three decades, and can no longer be heard singing high above the fields

Jays and yellowhammers (*inset*) contributed to the dawn chorus along the Whittingham Hospital Railway. (Courtesy of Peter Smith)

betwixt Grimsargh and Whittingham. It is sad they are no longer such a quintessential element and embodiment of all that was pure in the English countryside. Mozart was inspired by the countryside and birdsong as indeed were several of the great romantic composers of the nineteenth century, including Mahler and Beethoven. Poignantly, they gained creativity for their music by orchestrating images of the landscape and in the case of Beethoven the natural sound of birdsong. Perhaps without knowing it, those lovely sounds of the natural world were embedded in his psyche to be eventually transposed into his musical scores.

My composer/birdsong hypothesis is spurred for example by the abrupt staccato call of the perky and mischievous Cetti's warbler in the opening notes of Beethoven's Fifth Symphony. In the second movement of his Pastoral Symphony, itself a delightful musical rendition of the countryside, the scene by the brook is ineffably peaceful throughout albeit suitably interrupted by the timely inclusion of the songs of nightingale rendered by the flute, quail (oboe) and cuckoo (clarinet) towards the end of the movement. Here is one genius in awe of a whole class of prodigies, which prompts the question: was Ludwig Van Beethoven a twitcher? All the evidence suggests that perhaps he was. Nevertheless the sounds of the natural world inspired him to compose some of his finest thought-provoking music.

Unlike humans, birds do not sing because they are happy, though ultimately they might well be by stating their territory and finding a mate. My own experience during the early morning walk to Whittingham was that the robin punctuated the dawn with its melancholy overture, closely followed by the blackbird and song thrush. A blackbird singing is something really special and its flute-like notes are in total contrast to the song thrush, which repeats every syllable two or three times. No ghost trains along the Whittingham tracks, only a 'blackbird singing in the dead of night', tending to suggest that Paul McCartney got the ornithological content of the lyrics of his song 'Blackbird' technically correct! Likewise Respighi had a stroke of genius by using a recording of the classic European songster, the nightingale, in his musical rendition of *Pines of Rome*.

On the Whittingham line, however, there was one modest soloist along the track; the ubiquitous wren. The extraordinary loud aria from the tiny wren resonated throughout the woodland before disappearing again, only to take a further curtain call and perhaps even an encore before making way for the next soloist. On hearing a strange unfamiliar call in the woodland it was usually part of the great tit's extensive repertoire of more than forty calls, the most common of which sounded like it was calling for 'teacher, teacher, teacher!'

I listened carefully for the murmurings of starlings; this intriguing species was always an early riser, but was an excellent mimic and could even imitate the glorious call of the curlews that were common in the meadows alongside the track. The loud vibrating rattle produced by rapidly repeated blows of its strong bill upon a tree or branch represented the territorial claim of the great spotted woodpecker in a cluster of trees overhanging Savick Brook. In this avian chorus the woodpecker added his own

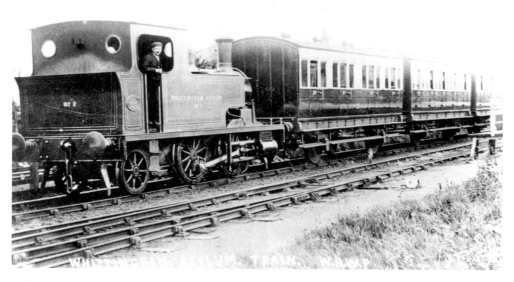

A final look into how it used to be – a pristine Barclay No. 2 with LYR passenger carriages at Grimsargh, *c.* 1920. (Hospital Archives)

touch of percussion, while the far-carrying laughing calls of the green woodpecker or 'yaffle', provided a comic interlude. Overhead the raven, a rare guest soloist during winter, made up the brass section with its instantly recognisable deep 'pruckpruck' trumpeting calls. The harsh rasping sound of jays made their presence known in the same copse, but their discord added little to the wondrous chorus while lapwings called out their other name of 'peewit' in a cacophony of rising chords and sounded absolutely great.

Further along the track a variety of warblers sang beautifully to establish their territories from deep within a railway cutting, and collectively made up a worthy ornithological chorus. Willow warblers with their liquid cadence descended the scales in their own special way, while the similar plumage of the chiffchaff was belied by its repetitive 'chiff-chaff' call – an obvious metaphor of the bird's name. The song of the garden warbler added its own touch of melodiousness whilst that of the similar blackcap was more strident. Nearby a yellowhammer gave a solo rendition that sounded like 'a little bit of bread and no cheese' along the embankment at Brabiner Lane. I somehow don't think it found either the bread or the cheese but sadly nowadays this bright yellow jewel of a bird is long gone from here, while the yellow wagtail that was abundant in fields alongside the track is virtually extinct throughout Lancashire. As a fitting finale, tawny owls gave their distinctive call before retiring to their own secret daytime roost. Having absorbed all of the splendid musicianship expressed in the dawn chorus, not to mention discord, one returned to the real world and a real treat, two rounds of toast and ham and eggs for breakfast in the hospital canteen!

Acknowledgements

In writing this social history I have drawn on primary and secondary sources detailed in the bibliography. It has been a privilege to share experiences with a host of helpful and interesting people. Accordingly I extend my sincere thanks to Andrew Mather and members of the Jesuit Community at Preston, the Preston Historical Society and Longridge and District History Society.

I am grateful to Wing Commander Alan Wilding for helpful comments and to Alan Castle, Gordon Biddle, Peter Fitton, Dorron Harper, Stan Withers, Peter Smith, Mark Bartlett, George Whiteman, and Richard and Mr H. C. Casserley, for the use of photographs. Furthermore I acknowledge the help and expertise of Mike Atherton, Alan Castle, Tom Heginbotham and Robert Gregson. Mrs Frances Wright, the widow of Mr Gilbert Wright, the last driver on the line, who spent most of his working life on the Whittingham engines, also to Syd Brown of Longridge and Mrs Ada Wild at Dixon's Farm, who also provided valued anecdotal information.

I acknowledge the help of staff at the National Archive, Kew, London; National Railway Museum, York; Harris Reference Library, Preston; and the Lancashire Record Office (LRO), who have offered advice and furnished valued sources of archived material. Newspaper and oral accounts have provided material for a light-hearted, retrospective look at the Victorian steam railway, though I am aware that unconfirmed anecdotal material is often almost impossible to rebut.

I have made every effort to trace copyright owners of illustrative and textual material, though this has sometimes proved very difficult. Therefore both the author and publisher wish to apologise if any acknowledgement has been omitted. Finally I would like to thank my publisher for making this new work possible.

Appendix

A Brief Chronological History of the Preston to Longridge and Whittingham Railways

Year	Name of event
1836	The Royal Assent is granted by Parliament to the Preston & Longridge Railway Company.
1840	The line opens and services commence between Longridge and Deepdale Street Stations – the latter being the initial terminus of the line. Initially, horse-haulage is adopted.
1846	The entire line is leased to the Fleetwood, Preston & West Riding Junction Railway (FP & WRJR).
1848	The first steam-hauled train runs on Whit Monday.
1850	A double-track extension now connects the existing line, a few hundred yards east of the Deepdale Street terminus at Deepdale Junction, with Maudland and thence onto the existing route into the Fylde, via the new Maudland (or 'Miley') tunnel. Freight traffic only is conveyed at this time.
1854	A new station is opened at what is successively to be named Gamull (or Gammer) Lane in 1854, Fulwood in 1856 and, ultimately, Ribbleton in 1900 (the latter not to be confused with the later Ribbleton Station that came to be situated nearby).
1856	The line is extended beyond Deepdale Street Station, with new stations being opened at Deepdale and Maudland Bridge, the latter being at the new end of the line and close to Preston town centre.
1863	A new station is opened at Ribbleton (not to be confused with the earlier built station that came to assume the name following closure of the later establishment).
1867	The LNWR & LYR Joint Committee assumes ownership and operation of the line from the FP & WRJR.
1868	The original 1863 Ribbleton Station is closed to all traffic.

1870   Grimsargh Station is opened for business, replacing the earlier structure located within the premises of the Plough Inn.

1872   A new station at Longridge is built adjacent to the Townley Arms Hotel.

1885   The installation is completed of the Maudland Curve that provided the direct link to Preston Station and facilitating railway connections to other railway lines to the south for the first time. Concurrently with this, Maudland Bridge Station is closed.

1889   The Whittingham Hospital Railway is opened and commences a passenger service connecting into the Longridge services.

1923   Following the Grouping, the London Midland & Scottish Railway assumes ownership of the PLR and operation of the line from the LNWR & LYR Joint Committee.

1948   Following Nationalisation, British Railways takes over operation of the PLR.

1930   After ninety years, passenger services are withdrawn from the entire line as from 2 June 1930, causing the closure of all stations to passengers – although freight and parcels traffic will survive for much longer.

1957   The Whittingham Hospital Railway is closed to all traffic; its passenger services having survived those on the 'main-line' by all of twenty-seven years!

1967   The withdrawal of freight facilities at Grimsargh and Longridge Stations, in November 1967, brings about the complete closure of the route beyond Courtaulds Sidings.

1980   Courtaulds Factory closes and, with it, the section of line between Courtaulds Sidings and Deepdale Junction.

1994   The withdrawal of the final coal trains serving Deepdale brings about the complete closure of the remaining operable section of the line.

Endnotes

1. See Ordnance Survey Map (1844), 6" to 1 mile, in LRO.
2. Anderson, M., *Family Structure in nineteenth-century Lancashire* (Cambridge University Press, 1971) p. 33.
3. Anderson, M., *Family Structure in nineteenth-century Lancashire* (Cambridge University Press, 1971) p. 24.
4. Livesey, J., *Staunch Teetotaller*, November, 1867, No. 11, p. 164.
5. *Preston Chronicle*, 30 January, 1869.
6. Parliamentary Papers, 1852–3, (855) XXXXVII Select Committee on Public Houses and Places of Public Entertainment, (Minutes of Evidence) Q6416.
7. Harrison, B., *Drink and the Victorians* (Keele University Press, 1994) p. 112.
8. Hunt, D., *A History of Preston* (Carnegie Publishing, 1992) p. 193.
9. Dennis, R., *English Industrial Cities of the nineteenth century* (Cambridge University Press) p. 30.
10. Savage, M., *The Dynamic of Working Class Politics* (Cambridge University Press, 1987) p. 126.
11. Joyce, P., *Work, Society and Politics* (Methuen Press, 1982) p. 292/4.
12. Flintoff, T., *Preston and Parliament* (Preston Reference Library, 1981) pp. 7–9.
13. Pelling, H., *Social Geography of British Elections* (McMillan, 1967) pp. 261–2.
14. *Preston Chronicle*, 22 February, 1865.
15. 'Life in Preston', *Preston Chronicle*, 11 February, 1865.
16. Rail 576, Item 1674, The National Archive, Kew.
17. Rail 576, Item 1882, The National Archive, Kew.
18. *Preston Guardian*, 18 October, 1947.

Bibliography

Primary Sources Held at The National Archive, Kew

Reference	Title	Covering Dates
Rail 1075/428	*Prospectus: Preston and Longridge Railway*	1835
ZPER 33/1	'Description of PLR' (*Railway Mag. Vol. 1*)	1836
ZPER 34/20	*Illustrated London News*	1852
Rail 576	*Minutes of Preston – Longridge Joint Committee*	1866–1889
MT 6/482/6	*Grimsargh Level Crossing*	1887
Rail 329	*Whittingham Railway*	1887–1957
AN 155/14	*Preston – Longridge*	1964–1968

Primary Sources Held at the Lancashire Record Office

LRO PDR58 Enclosure Awards, 1835.

LRO DDC1/1183 Original correspondence of P & L Railway, 1836.

LRO DDCL1187/2 Notice of Meeting to raise Money for P & L Rly, 1840.

LRO PDR243 Map of P & L Railway showing townships, 1835.

LRO DDX189/15 Original plan of route of WHR, 1884.

LRO DDX189/16 Parliamentary procedures – plan of WHR, 1885.

LRO 3GTUD/188 Aerial photographs.

LRO HRW1/6-1/21 Reports of Committee of Visitors 1883–1947 & Whittingham Hospital Management Committees.

Secondary Sources

Books

Biddle, G., *The Railways Around Preston – A Historical Review* (Foxline Publishing, 1989).

Clinker, *Railway History Sources* (AO4CC1.)

Edwards C., *Railway records: A Guide to Sources* (Kew, 2001).

Gregson, R., *Lancashire & Yorkshire Railway Around Preston* (Atkinson Publications Ltd, 2011)

Gregson, R., *London & Northwestern Railway Around Preston* (Atkinson Publications Ltd, 2012)

Hindle D., *Grimsargh: The Story of a Lancashire Village* (Carnegie Publishing, 2002).

Hindle D., *All Stations to Longridge* (Amberley Publishing, 2010).

Parker, N., *The Preston and Longridge Railway* (Oakwood Press, 1972).

Rush, R. W., *The Lancashire and Yorkshire Railway and its Locomotives, 1846–1923* (London: 1949).

Till, J. M., *A History of Longridge and its People* (Carnegie Publishing, 1993).

Voice, D., *Hospital Tramways and Railways* (Adam Gordon, 2005).

Periodicals

Aubertin, C., 'Solving a Victorian Problem', *Steam World* (October 2006).

Casserley, H. C., 'The Whittingham Railway', *Railway Magazine* (May 1957).

Cliff, A., 'Ride on the Whittingham Hospital Railway', *Steam World* (December 1996).

Hindle, D., 'Grimsargh Junction, Change For Whittingham', *Steam Days* (May 2004).

Hindle, D., 'Change for Whittingham Junction', *Steam World* (August 2011).

Jones, N., 'Affray at Whittingham', *Railway Magazine* (May, 1958).

Jones, N., 'The Whittingham Railway', *Country Life* (6 June, 1963).

Jones, N., 'The Whittingham Hospital Railway', *Railway Bylines* (January, 2001).

Perkins, T. R., 'The Whittingham Railway', *Railway Magazine* (April 1934).